Leading
At The Top

Leading At The Top

Requirements for Senior Executive Effectiveness

A Framework for Developing and Assessing Senior Leaders

John R. Hook

iUniverse, Inc.
New York Lincoln Shanghai

Leading At The Top
Requirements for Senior Executive Effectiveness

Copyright © 2006 by John R. Hook

iUniverse books may be ordered through booksellers or by contacting:

iUniverse
2021 Pine Lake Road, Suite 100
Lincoln, NE 68512
www.iuniverse.com
1-800-Authors (1-800-288-4677)

ISBN-13: 978-0-595-38439-6 (pbk)
ISBN-13: 978-0-595-82817-3 (ebk)
ISBN-10: 0-595-38439-0 (pbk)
ISBN-10: 0-595-82817-5 (ebk)

Printed in the United States of America

For Carol, Cathy, and Mark
(Only they could know why)

Contents

Acknowledgments

Many people contributed to this book. Some shared their most creative ideas, others their technical skills, and many their encouragement and support.

- Professors Frank Sherwood and Bob Biller of the University of Southern California taught me much that has influenced my thinking: Frank on the nature and practice of senior leadership, and Bob on the management of change.

- Dr. Pete Petersen, Senior Professor of Management at Johns Hopkins University: A long-time friend, accomplished author, and true expert on the teaching and practice of leadership—who reviewed the manuscript, contributed many ideas, and was supportive throughout the project.

- Professor Charlie Beitz, my colleague at both the Army War College and Mount St. Mary's University. Charlie and I have been friends for many years and collaborators on numerous projects. He is a deep and creative thinker particularly on the subject of leadership, and I confess to stealing many of his ideas.

- Professor Bill Forgang, also a friend and colleague at Mount St. Mary's University. Bill is the smartest person I've ever known in the area of business strategy. His thinking had an important impact on this book, as did his continuing interest and support.

- Jeff Olson, my editor on two books at Velocity Business Publishing. Jeff is a great friend and valuable resource on anything related to management literature and the business of publishing. Jeff knows it all—and is so generous in sharing his expertise.

- Alice Barr and Elizabeth Sugg of Prentice Hall. They had faith in this project, got me started, and helped throughout with advice, interest, and friendship.

- Ronald Houseal, a graduate of the Mount Saint Mary's MBA program and an outstanding former student of mine—who very graciously allowed me to use portions of his master's thesis on the Johnson & Johnson Tylenol Crisis.

- Father Henry Haske, a Jesuit priest and a lifelong friend. He gave me lots of moral support—plus expert advice and editorial assistance with the sections on the Catholic Church Crisis and Pope John XXIII.

- Connie Pryor, a friend and savvy judge of writing and content. Connie commented on early drafts and stayed in touch with helpful advice throughout the project.

- Becky Brown, secretary of the Business Department at Mount St. Mary's, a great collaborator on previous books, a valuable source of advice and assistance on this one until she retired, and a strong supporter of the book long after that.

- Sandy Kauffman, administrator of the Mount St. Mary's MBA program, who took over when Becky retired and provided the necessary skills I lacked to see the project through. Sandy does everything with superb professionalism and good cheer.

- Joann Woy, superb free lance editor—and cheerleader for her clients. Talented and easy to work with, Annie did the final edit. She has an uncanny ability to improve your writing while still honoring the idiosyncrasies of your style.

- Dr. Moshe Yair Levy, M.D. of Johns Hopkins Hospital. I could never say enough about Dr. Levy. He knows why he's listed here. Fantastic guy!!

- My children: Mark, Carol, and Cathy, and their spouses: Gail, Cameron, and Fritz. All are always totally supportive of anything that anyone in the family does. Their continuous interest, encouragement, and support (through some difficult days in my life during the writing of this book) is gratefully appreciated. Great people, all!!

- My grandchildren: John, Brian, Katie, Matthew, Patrick, Colleen, Kelly, and Caroline. They are a constant source of love and inspiration for me. Their parents are always amused when I say this—but these guys truly have no downside!!

- Finally, I must mention my wife, Pat. She was always a one-person cheering section for each member of our family, and she remains with us in spirit, inspiring us to do our best. As I wrote this, and two previous books, I frequently found myself imagining her comments: "Too wordy, John"—and that has made it a much better book. God Bless!!

Chapter 1

Introduction

This is a book about leading at the top of the organization. Its premise is that leadership at the most senior level is a unique experience calling for a special set of professional characteristics, personal qualities, and technical competencies. The book focuses precisely on those characteristics, qualities, and competencies.

The book is intended to serve a wide audience: senior leaders and those who report directly to them, aspiring executives, and those responsible for selecting and appointing top leaders in all kinds of organizations. It should also be of interest to those who teach and train leaders, and to consultants on organizational effectiveness.

The ideas here have been derived from five decades of association with the subject of leadership: doing it at lower levels, watching senior leaders do it (as a direct report or consultant), and teaching leadership to graduate students and senior managers. Since one's experience has a bearing on credibility and point of view, the reader should know mine at the outset.

I feel very fortunate to have had three diverse career experiences contributing to my background in leadership: Army officer for 29 years, academic for 22 years, and management consultation throughout my teaching career.

My army service included the following assignments: Battalion Commander; G3 (Plans and Operations Officer) for all U.S. Army Air Defense Forces in NATO; Executive Officer (Chief of Staff) of a 7,000-man separate infantry brigade in Vietnam; Group Commander of a 3,500-man air defense missile group in Germany; and duty with three research and development organizations in Washington (Defense Nuclear Agency, Ballistic Missile Defense Program Office, and Office of the Chief of Research and Development of the Army). Also, while in the service, I had the opportunity to teach at West Point and Chair the Command, Leadership, and Management Department at the U.S. Army War College.

After retiring from the Army in 1980, I chaired the Department of Business and Economics at Mount St. Mary's College (now University) for 12 years, then remained a faculty member there for an additional 10 years, teaching undergraduate and graduate courses in management. During that time, I also conducted hundreds of management seminars and provided other consulting services for public, private, and non-profit organizations—most for senior-level managers.

What I know about senior-level leadership, what I write here, is the product of what I have learned from others through reading, observing senior leaders, and interacting with them on the job, in the classroom, and in the boardroom. I see their role as unique and vital:

- They represent the organization and are fully exposed. Everything they do and say is watched and assessed both internally and externally.

- They are the final decision makers and are accountable for all actions and events on their watch. Their reputations are built on a day-to-day and decision-to-decision basis.

- They are the chief representatives of the organization's strategy. Thus, their words and behavior shape the attitudes and actions of everyone else.

My thesis is that it takes four things to effectively lead at the top: Certain professional characteristics and personal qualities, the ability to manage change, the ability to manage crises, and a willingness to accept risk. The material is thus depicted as a four-part skill set in the *Senior Executive Leadership Model* (next page) and described in four parts or modules in the text. The model reflects that the organization's strategy is the key outcome of the leader's skill set. That strategy drives all execution actions. The feedback loop reflects the need to continually reexamine three things when problems arise with execution: objectives, the leader's skill set, and the strategy—until successful execution is achieved. The thrust of the four parts or modules is briefly summarized here.

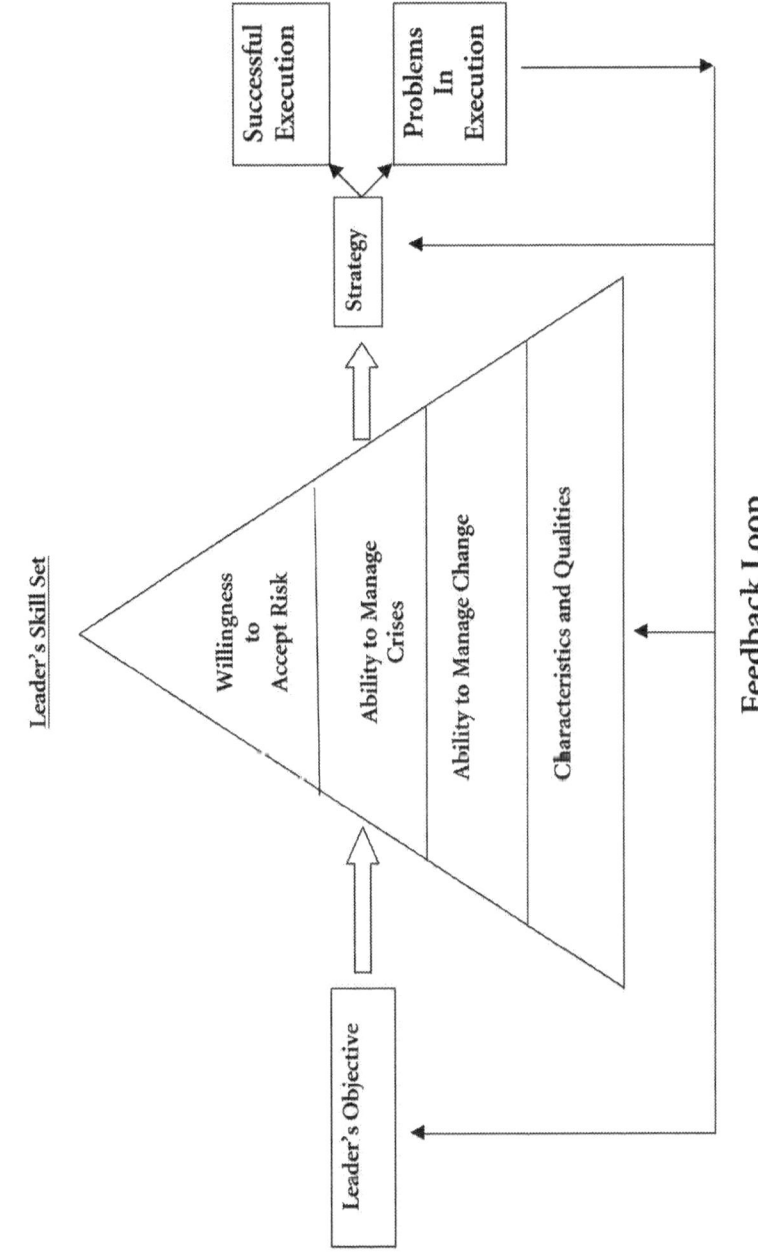

Senior Executive Leadership Model

Leader's Skill Set

Willingness to Accept Risk

Ability to Manage Crises

Ability to Manage Change

Characteristics and Qualities

Strategy

Successful Execution

Problems In Execution

Leader's Objective

Feedback Loop

Part I: Critical Characteristics and Qualities

Nineteen characteristics and qualities are identified as critical to effective performance. Some are important to leaders at every level, and some apply only at the senior level. Here, I discuss why each applies to the senior leader. To illustrate and validate points, I rely on widely known leaders, using both contemporary and historical examples. There are three reasons for this approach: (1) These individuals all qualify as senior leaders; (2) we know the facts since their records are well documented; and (3) using them permits an economy of language since their deeds are known to most readers. And one final point: Though I discuss each characteristic and quality separately, this list must be considered an interdependent and comprehensive package that defines the executive. Having 80% of these characteristics and qualities is not good enough. A blend of all is needed for full effectiveness.

Part II: Ability to Manage Change

Leading implies movement. Strong leaders seek to carry their organizations to higher ground. This means change—threatening to many and normally resisted by some. An awareness of change, sensitivity to its impact, and attention to the task of facilitating change are requirements for top leadership. Planning change has been a specialty area in my consulting practice for over twenty years, and in this module I identify, and illustrate with case examples, nine principles for facilitating change that I have found helpful to client organizations.

Part III: Ability to Manage Crises

Senior leaders have important roles to play at all times. But in times of crisis, the top leader's role becomes dominant. It is during crises that they earn their pay, and their reputations are largely made by how they handle crises. The book uses six examples of organizations in crisis to develop a set of twenty-six principles for managing crises: Johnson & Johnson's Tylenol Crisis (1982); Corporate Malfeasance Crisis: The Business Scandals of 2002; U2 Spy Plane Crisis (1960); Cuban Missile Crisis (1962); Memogate: The Crisis at CBS (September 2004); and The Catholic Church Sexual Abuse Crisis (2001–2002).

Part IV: **Willingness to Accept Risk**

Much has been written about risk reduction and managing risk. My focus here is different—it is on the top leader's willingness to *accept* risk. This willingness to accept risk is central to the senior executive's capacity to lead. Individuals can have all the other qualifications for senior leadership, but if they are not willing to accept the risk, they will not take the actions necessary in troubled times, when strong leadership is most necessary. Even though they have the capability to do what is required, they will fail to take action through lack of nerve. A variety of well-known historical case examples are used in this section to illustrate this point—examples of various kinds of risks in different of types of organizations.

The four parts must be considered interdependent, since all four components of the skill set are essential to the leader. However, each part has been written as a stand-alone module that can be studied out-of-sequence if this better meets the needs of individual readers, teachers, or trainers.

To assist users, the following features have been incorporated into the book:

- *Chapter Objectives and Summaries*

- *Key Points*: Summary statements placed in the margin

- *Quotations*: Validating statements by great thinkers, leaders, and authorities to emphasize and strengthen important points

- *Your Turn Questions*: Questions placed at key intervals to help readers reflect on the material and relate it to their experiences

- *Application Exercises*: Self-assessment tests at the end of each module

- *Suggestions for Teachers and Trainers* (in an Appendix): Ideas and advice for classroom use, including individual and group projects

Major bookstores are filled with books on leadership. So, how is this book different? What does it offer that other books lack? The book is distinct in three ways:

- *Focus*: The book focuses specifically on *senior* leadership. It does not, as many books do, blur the distinction between senior leadership and the task of leading at lower levels.

- *Comprehensiveness*: Many serious leadership books concentrate on some single leadership concept (e.g., transactional leadership, emotional leadership, followership). They are very useful books that add to the body of knowledge. The strength of these books lies in their depth; their weakness is typically a lack of breadth. This book is different in that it provides a comprehensive framework or lens to view the senior leadership role, which includes all important elements of the job.

- *Simplicity*: Most books on leadership are too long and too detailed for the busy people likely to read them. This book provides just enough detail to make its points.

Think briefly on the world of organizations that you see today: governments, businesses, and non-profits. Consider the changes confronting all of them, and the crises facing many. You are sure to conclude that the need for quality senior leadership has never been greater. My hope is that this book will help some present and future leaders, and those who serve them, to better fill the void.

Part I

Critical Characteristics and Qualities

"The buck stops here."

—President Harry Truman

This module is designed to help the reader develop a comprehensive system for evaluating executive qualifications and performance. The material is divided into two chapters: Chapter 2 (Characteristics) identifies ten professional characteristics of an effective senior leader. Chapter 3 (Qualities) identifies nine essential personal qualities. Taken collectively, these nineteen characteristics and qualities represent a tool to evaluate senior leaders and to aid in personal development.

Each chapter begins with stated learning objectives and ends with summary points. At the end of the discussion of each characteristic or competency a "Your Turn" question is posed to help you reflect on the material and relate it to your experience.

The best way to navigate this module is to first read the chapters and reflect on the "Your Turn" questions. Next, review the chapter objectives and summaries. And finally, complete the application exercises at the end of the module.

What result should you expect? Certainly not simply memory of the characteristics and qualities—you'll always have access to them. Rather, you should have greater confidence in your ability to use the nineteen characteristics and qualities as a comprehensive framework or lens to view and evaluate other leaders and improve your own capabilities.

Chapter 2

Characteristics

Objectives

- Recognize senior leadership as a unique role.
- Learn ten professional characteristics to evaluate executive qualifications and performance.
- Develop tools to critique senior leaders.
- Develop tools for personal self-development.

This chapter discusses the following ten professional characteristics considered essential to senior leader effectiveness:

- A Sense of Context
- Perspective: Know Their Role as Senior Leaders
- Vision—and a Passion for Purpose
- External Orientation: Global/Interorganizational
- Strategic Thinkers
- Understand the Work of the Organization
- Communicate Effectively
- Attract and Retain Talented People
- Attend to Management and Institution Building
- Allocate Resources Effectively

A Sense of Context

This characteristic provides insights into the setting: the organization's unique characteristics and current situation—the reality with which the executive must deal. Five issues are used here to highlight the importance of a sense of context:

> The context often dictates the action.

- The degree of environmental and organizational turbulence.

- The organization's stage of development.

- The existence of power centers of professionals within the organization.

- The managerial diversity characteristic of non-profit and government organizations.

- The organization's culture.

> "I tend to think of the differences between leaders and managers as the difference between those who master the context and those who surrender to it."
>
> —Warren Bennis

Turbulence is always an issue of first importance. Wars, recessions, and tough competition come instantly to mind. These are global events that impact profoundly on the leader's task. But internal turbulence can complicate things as well: Warring factions, faulty structures, and dysfunctional cultures can play havoc with organizational effectiveness and thus demand skilled leadership. A clearly articulated strategy is one of the best leverage mechanisms for guiding the organization through turbulent times.

The organization's stage of development is also a key issue. Organizations are dynamic in nature. As they proceed through various stages of growth, they need different types of leaders. Early on, at start-up, there can be a good deal of flailing around. Creativity in the leader is invaluable at this moment in the organization's history. Then, as things settle down and missions get established, the need for high creativity diminishes and skills at building the organization (hiring, staffing, establishing policy) become dominant, calling for a different type leader. When everything is up and running, still another type of leader is in demand: a person skilled at "making the trains run on time." Finally, when it becomes necessary to make the trains run in a different direction, a good change agent is needed at the helm.

A third context issue involves the distribution of power within the organization. Certain kinds of organizations have heavy power centers of professionals: individuals who do the essential work of the organization but are not part of the management system. Doctors in hospitals and professors in universities are examples of this phenomenon. These professionals don't want to manage, but they know their value, and they want their way. Dwight Eisenhower, on assuming the presidency of Columbia University, made the mistake of referring to the faculty as employees of the university and was promptly corrected by a faculty member saying: We are not employees of the university; we are the university. The power of professional groups can be very intimidating, and not every senior leader is comfortable in an environment with such influential stakeholders.

A fourth context issue exists in non-profit organizations and in government. Non-profits typically rely on the services of volunteers, many of whom also have management responsibilities within the organization. Government organizations have three types of managers: elected, appointed, and careerists—each with different mandates. Elected officials need to be conscious of the platform that got them elected. Careerists must function as the sources of institutional memory and expertise. Appointed officials need to be the bridge between elected officials and careerists. Such features greatly add to the complexity of the senior leader's task. Many have found the move from corporate leadership to the ambiguous world of non-profits and government to be very uncomfortable, and some have failed to meet the challenge.

Finally, organizational culture must be considered when assessing context. Organizations differ profoundly in culture. In some, a rigid hierarchy prevails and the leader is relatively free to point the way. Most military organizations and many corporations fit this model. But in settings where power is distributed by virtue of technical expertise or professional entities, such autocratic leadership is not possible. Thus, as a part of their overall sense of context, leaders must look to the culture for guidance on how to proceed.

The point here is: Upon assuming top leadership positions, executives need to be conscious of the context issues—and ask themselves critical context questions, such as:

- Are we in troubled times or in easier, more predictable circumstances?
- Is an unacceptable level of internal turbulence present, and what can I do about it?
- What is our stage of growth, and what must I contribute at this point to be effective?
- What is unique about our structure and membership that calls for special handling on my part, and exactly how must I deal with that?
- What do we need to do to be successful, and what must I do to move us forward?
- How do I move us forward in the culture that exists here?

These are some of the questions that top executives must ask to find their proper role. And, ideally, even before accepting the top position, the individual should ask: What will need to be done here, and will I be happy and effective in my leadership role?

Your Turn

Think of a situation in which you saw context ignored or poorly handled. What was the impact?

Perspective: Know Their Role as Senior Leaders

The top executive does many things that lower managers do not do. And, even in functions and tasks common to all levels, the senior leader does them differently. Perspective on top executive roles and how they differ from those of lower level leaders is vital.

Some of the major role differences are identified below.

> "Leaders are people who do the right thing; managers are people who do things right. Both roles are crucial, but they differ profoundly. I often observe people in top positions doing the wrong things well."
>
> —Warren Bennis

Lower Management vs. Top Executive Roles

Moving higher requires changing role perceptions.

Lower Management	Top Executive
Sees the parts	Sees the whole
Looks in	Looks out
Agency perspective	Global perspective
Emphasis: doing things right	Emphasis: doing right things
Champions causes	Mediates disputes
Task oriented	Goal oriented
Industrious	Thoughtful
Short-term planner	Long-term planner
Production oriented	Policy oriented
Recruits for jobs	Attracts talent

Lower Management	*Top Executive*
Works in present	Works in future
Observes operations	Studies environment
Product oriented	Process oriented
Recommends	Decides
Provides staff work	Utilizes staff work

Leaders with the top executive perspective are more likely to ask themselves the following kinds of revealing questions:

- Are we in the right business? Are our goals the right goals for us?
- How can I create an organizational culture and climate that will attract the kinds of talent we need?
- What policies will help us develop and retain top talent?

The executive's perspective is enhanced also through recognition of the importance of political behavior at senior levels. To a degree, all leaders practice both political behavior and managerial behavior, but the executive's need for political behavior is much more dominant. Some differences in political and managerial behavior are identified below.

Political vs. Managerial Behavior

Managerial	*Political*
Goals stated clearly	Goals not fully disclosed
Candid communications	Veiled communications
Predictable	Unpredictable
High accountability	Distributed accountability
Well-defined roles	Shifting and overlapping roles
Staffing by competence	Staffing by buddy system
Cooperative	Competitive
Disciplined	Freewheeling

Executives with the necessary political perspective are more likely to ask the following types of questions:

- How much of our plans should I reveal? When? To whom?

- Would there be an advantage to having more than one person, department, or agency responsible for this particular critical task?

- Who should I pick for my chief of staff—an experienced hand, or a friend who understands the way I like to work?

One final thought: It is not enough for the executive to simply possess perspective. One of the challenges at the top is to get subordinates to think two or three levels above the job they are doing. Such education is important: to help subordinates serve the boss better, to develop them for future responsibilities, and to ensure each part of the organization is commonly guided.

Your Turn

Examine the list of top executive roles. In which role would you be weakest? What can you do to develop in that role?

Vision—and a Passion for Purpose

There is a vast difference between management and leadership. It is often possible to be a good manager by having the capacity to assemble a great team and direct their activities with skill. But leadership is different. To lead, you must want to do something with the organization—to take it to higher ground. You must have a vision, a purpose. And, if you expect others to follow, you must have passion for that purpose.

Vision and purpose can't be faked. We know it when we see it. And it is usually simply stated. Some examples from history:

It's the "vision thing" that drives the strategy.

- Churchill—Defeat Hitler
- Martin Luther King—"The Dream"
- Ronald Reagan—Less government, more defense, fewer taxes
- Lee Iacocca—Save the Chrysler Corporation

"The secret of success is constancy to purpose."

—Benjamin Disraeli

- Steve Jobs (founder of Apple Computer)—Build a user-friendly computer

Vision has a magic effect on leadership. It is now several years after the disaster of September 11, 2001. Prior to that awful event, President George W. Bush had provided the country with a not unreasonable set of goals: lower taxes, education reform, improved military, etc. He was barely elected, and most of the country was not very excited about his agenda. He seemed at times a weak and uncertain leader. But September 11 changed the nation's impression of him. Bush found his true purpose: defeat terrorism. And he found his voice: "We will not falter and we will not fail." Of course, the event demanded a strong statement of purpose. Further, we don't know how this will all play out in the end. But let's not minimize or lose the lesson of the President's achievement at that particular moment in history. Many in his place would not have so quickly grasped the essence of the situation and set the nation's course. Most who heard him would agree his statement of purpose focused a stunned nation. His passion for that purpose was contagious because his words matched the feelings of his countrymen. His success long-term will be judged by history (let's all hope favorably). But, at that moment, we witnessed an important short-term success in vision and purpose, and it serves us here to reflect on that experience.

Every senior executive cannot be expected to find such dramatic events to spark vision. But each must be a visionary—must ask, upon assuming the position: What is the purpose of this organization, its reason for being? What's my purpose here? What do I want to accomplish? How do I wish to transform the organization on my watch? What specific priorities must I emphasize to accomplish my purpose? Finding the key priority areas and focusing on them with laser-beam intensity is essential to success. It tells the senior leader what programs to push and how to use his or her time effectively.

> ## Your Turn
>
> What is the most effective vision statement you have encountered in your organizational experience?

External Orientation: Global/Interorganizational

> The outside world will bite you if you don't keep your eye on it continually.

Knowledge of the work of the organization and management of the organization internally are important, but not sufficient at senior levels. The senior leader must recognize that, in most cases, the organization's survival and prosperity depend on players and factors in the external environment of the organization (e.g., suppliers, competitors, advisors, boards of directors, and economic and technological factors).

> "Keeping a little ahead of conditions is one of the secrets of business; the trailer seldom goes far."
>
> —Charles Schwab

The role of senior leadership is to link the organization to that external world. Of course, there are people to help with boundary spanning activities. But it is the chief executive who provides the direction and motivation to keep the outside world on the front burner and to ensure that the necessary linkages are made to external forces.

The importance of this external orientation is the reason for many of the qualities sought in top executives: that they be multi-roled people with linkages to many worlds, environmental scanners alert to sensitive external factors, good boundary spanners and coalition builders who can make the appropriate connections to the external world, and that they have the wisdom and capacity to pick the right people to help them.

Presidents again provide both positive and negative examples:

- One of Jimmy Carter's biggest mistakes was forming his key staff largely with what became known as the "Georgia Mafia"—a young group, skilled in managing political campaigns, but totally inexperienced in the ways of Washington or the world. Having no clear vision for the country, and a staff unable to help him deal with Congress and the outside world, Carter's administration floundered from the start and was ultimately unsuccessful.

- George Bush (senior) was by nature a gregarious man capable of easy friendships with foreign leaders. He used his inclination and talent to reach out in untroubled times. Consequently, when trouble struck in the form of problems with Iraq, he was able to quickly build a powerful coalition for the Gulf War.

- John Kennedy too had a flair for matters international, and a keen sense for influencing relevant players in the external environment. During the Cuban Missile Crisis in 1962, he picked with great care his emissaries to inform foreign governments of his intention to blockade Cuba, and used both personal messages and various supplementary methods to communicate with his adversary (Khrushchev) throughout the crisis. When informed by his press secretary that certain newspapers had gotten wind of his plans and were about to publish them prematurely, he recognized that he needed to personally call the publishers with whom he had maintained good personal relations.

Successful chief executives today know that the solutions to most organizational problems lie outside the boundaries of the organization—that their major challenge is not in managing a single organization but in hooking multiple organizations together. Consequently, even in a very calm and predictable environment, an external orientation is important. In the turbulent environments experienced by most organizations today, it is essential to be proactive in dealing with and influencing that outside world.

Your Turn

Can you think of any organization that was blindsided because of a lack of attention to its external environment? What happened?

Strategic Thinkers

The effective executive must have the ability to think strategically and thus assess decision options in light of the way the organization competes. Every decision must be made consistent with the overall strategy. Such a capacity requires the ability to see the organization as a total system with interconnected and interdependent components (e.g., technology, structure, people), processes (e.g., planning, decision-making), and functions (e.g., personnel, finance, research). It requires also a comprehensive and realistic grasp of the broader environment within which the organization must perform, and with which it must continually interact. What is required is a strategic way of thinking

> "You've got to think about 'big things' while you're doing small things, so that all the small things go in the right direction."
>
> —Alvin Toffler

that consistently uses a common strategy-related decision-making lens to view all decision options.

> Strategy must drive all policies and actions.

The relationship between *vision, purpose, values,* and *strategy* is important. To have *vision* is to see the organization's ideal *purpose*: what it should seek to give to society by way of goods and services. Visionary leaders have an image of what the organization can do for the world. *Purpose* is always guided by the *values* of the leader and ultimately of all organization members.

Strategy is the plan to achieve the organization's *purpose*. Effective visioning leads to sound strategy, which includes defining missions and establishing objectives, acquiring resources, designing structures, and setting policy and procedures—all in pursuit of *purpose*.

The organization's *strategy* defines the way in which it will compete in the marketplace. It includes all matters relevant to how the organization will differentiate itself: price, product quality, service standards—in short, how it plans to achieve a high level of performance.

The effective senior leader attends personally to the design and clear articulation of strategy because strategy should guide all subsequent decisions, activities, and behaviors.

The notion of strategy driving everything else is so important that I'd like to illustrate the concept with two personal examples.

- *Example #1—An Army Example*

In the late 1960s and early 1970s I served as a battalion commander and later a group commander in the army's air defense command in Germany. Our purpose was to provide air defense missile protection for the NATO ground forces. Our strategy statements always rightly emphasized the need to maintain a high state of operational readiness: the task of keeping missile systems operational and capable of moving in support of mobile ground forces. Such a strategy should have driven, and at times did drive us to train intensely for the night movement of units: displacing them, getting them up and running in a new location, and establishing communications with supported forces. However, at times we let ourselves depart from that strategy due to other, less important concerns. Night movements of heavy equipment are dangerous; they lead to accidents. We sometimes became so preoccupied with preventing accidents that we discouraged mobility training by rewarding low accident records in lieu of high operational capabilities. In effect, we were deviating from the strategy of optimizing operational readiness, with predictably negative results.

- *Example #2—A College Example*

I taught for over 20 years at a small college in Maryland. It's about 60 miles west of Baltimore, 70 miles north of Washington, D.C., and just 20 miles north of Frederick, the second largest city in Maryland and a growing community.

A portion of the college's strategy (how it competes) is to become known as the place in Frederick where one goes to study business. That element of strategy should and did drive a variety of its actions and policies:

- *Facilities*: There were several colleges offering business programs in Frederick. To compete, our college needed to establish classroom facilities in Frederick, and it did that.

- *Programs*: Undergraduate business offerings were expanded to include an accelerated degree-completion program in business for adults and a weekend program in partnership with a local community college. In addition, the existing MBA program was redesigned (to an accelerated mode) to make it more competitive, and was offered both in Frederick and at the main campus.

- *Organization*: The Frederick operation was placed under an on-site dean charged with being the local representative for all Frederick programs.

The jury is still out on the success of this endeavor. But a good start has been made, and the future looks promising if the leadership continues to let the strategy drive *all* actions, policies, and activities. But the college must be careful: Example #1 shows what can happen when an organization departs from its strategy.

Your Turn

Can you think of an organization that acted in a way that was not in keeping with its values? What was the impact?

Understand the Work of the Organization

At first thought, it might appear that a knowledge of the "nuts and bolts" aspects of an organization is unnecessary for top executives. It's tempting to think that the range of their concerns leaves little time for involvement with technical matters at the heart of the organization. Nothing could be further from the truth!

Particularly in the wide range of organizations engaged in knowledge-based work, it is critical for the senior leader to be thoroughly familiar with the technology of the organization: what it does, what it produces, and how. Cutting-edge decisions cannot be made without such knowledge. Thus, the point of decision will always be with the person who knows, and that had better be the top executive. Executives also need other important types of information and knowledge (e.g., management functions and processes; the players and factors in the organization's external environments). But a grasp of every other relevant area will not compensate for a lack of knowledge of the business of the enterprise, the work of the organization.

> He who knows decides.

> "Competence goes beyond words. It's the leader's ability to say it, plan it, and do it in such a way that others know that you know how—and know they want to follow you."
>
> —John C. Maxwell

Two cases on film, used extensively in management training for over twenty years, make this point well. The first is an NBC White Paper titled *Iacocca: An American Portrait*. In this hour-long film, Tom Brokaw (then NBC anchor) follows and interviews Lee Iacocca (then CEO of Chrysler) during a heated labor dispute in the mid-1980s. During a limo ride with Brokaw, Iacocca mentions that a few years earlier he had been fired as president of Ford Motor Company. In a reflective moment, he tells Brokaw that, after the firing, he had a whole summer to think about what he wanted to do with his life. He said he had a lot of offers from other companies—but *cars* were what he knew, and that Chrysler was the only game in town. By that statement, Iacocca demonstrated that he knew a lot more than the car industry: He understood the importance of knowing his business, the work of his organization.

The second case is depicted on a portion of the film, *In Search of Excellence*, based on the popular and influential book by Peters and Waterman, written in the 1980s. The clip of interest shows a very young Steve Jobs in his office during the early and very successful days at Apple Computer, which he had founded. Steve Jobs, in discussing leaders, said: "Do you know who the great leaders are? They are the great individual contributors, who never ever wanted to manage—but knew they had to because no one else could do it as well." Jobs was coming at this from the perspective of high-tech organizations (and probably Bill Gates would echo Job's view). In such environments, it is perhaps obvious that in-depth knowledge of the firm's product and process technologies is essential to making sound decisions. But research on a wide range of organizations confirms that it applies equally to most fields: non-profits, fire departments, police departments, military organizations, and universities— you name it.

Over the years, I have had the opportunity to observe many senior leaders in business, government, education, and the military. I always made it a point to note the degree to which they met this knowledge criteria and how it influenced their style and effectiveness. Without exception, those with deep knowledge of the work of their organization were able to lead more forcefully, confidently, and effectively. They could draw information from diverse stakeholders and challenge staff assumptions. They recognized they didn't always have the right answers, but they were confident they could ask the right questions. They seemed to think of themselves less as problem solvers and more as problem discoverers or lightning rods for the organization.

In summary, knowledge of the work of the organization is a must for senior leaders. Vision cannot be conceptualized without such knowledge. Further, the leader without knowledge quickly becomes irrelevant in the organization's decision process. Knowledge is power—he who knows decides!

Your Turn

Do you believe that a leader who is very effective in one type of organization can be equally effective in a very different type organization? Or, does your experience validate the point made in this book: that a leader must know the work of the organization to be effective?

Communicate Effectively

It is not enough to have a vision—to simply know where to go and what to do. The educative role of executives is critical. They must communicate the vision in ways that will influence others to sign on.

Good communication skills are not always measured by the eloquence of the speaker. Of course, all other things being equal, eloquence is a plus. Who can listen to the wartime speeches of Churchill or Franklin Roosevelt, or the Cold War inaugural address of John Kennedy and not be inspired? These men literally mobilized the language to inspire millions.

| Leaders communicate in multiple ways. | However, eloquence is not the sole measure of effectiveness, or even an essential element. What seems more important is a manner and language that touches one's | "Think like a wise man but communicate in the language of the people."

—William Butler Yeats |

various constituencies. Think of Harry Truman, Dwight Eisenhower, and George W. Bush (in the immediate aftermath of September 11). All three must be considered marginal public speakers. But often sincerity and clarity are more important than eloquence. Those qualities will carry the day when coupled with a keen sense of timing and media: knowing when, how often, in what way to tap in, and even who should speak the message (it need not always be the top executive).

Further, speech is not the only mechanism for communication. Senior leaders "speak" in many ways. Their body language says much. Whom they choose to consult also sends important messages. And, whenever they make a decision consistent with their vision and strategy, they communicate their most important message.

Regardless of the mechanism, the overarching goal of communications is to persuade multiple constituencies of the nature and worthiness of the leader's vision. The vision's power cannot be overestimated. Neglecting to sell it is always fatal.

It should also be noted that good listening skills are an important component of effective communications. Listening is essential to building networks designed to yield diverse views on complex issues. The key executive action here is climate setting. Senior leaders can be intimidating, so the trick is to establish a climate that encourages people to talk—to give the leader both good and bad news.

Your Turn

What are your major strengths and weaknesses as a communicator? What could you do to strengthen yourself in this area?

Attract and Retain Talented People

Few "one person" management systems exist today, none in high-knowledge type organizations. Though top leaders must understand the work of their organization, it is not necessary (and likely impossible) that they have all the technical smarts in the organization. Certainly, they cannot be expected to have the intellectual and manual dexterity needed to do all tasks efficiently and effectively. Especially in the task of developing a vision for the organization, the leader needs to collaborate extensively, both to gain knowledge (no one can have all the necessary knowledge) and to begin the process of building commitment to the vision. Thus, building staff becomes one of the essential tasks of the executive. Yet, it is often so poorly done. The late Peter Drucker, arguably this country's most experienced management author and consultant, has written: "By and large, executives make poor promotion and staffing decisions. By all accounts, their batting average is no better than .333: At most one-third of such decisions turn out right; one-third are minimally effective; and one-third are outright failures."

> "If anything goes bad, I did it. If anything goes semi-good, then we did it. If anything goes real good, then you did it. That's all it takes to get people to win football games for you."
>
> —Bear Bryant

> Getting and keeping the right people is the leader's most challenging task.

No executive could feel comfortable with such a record. So what does it take to do it right? Three skills are suggested here: The ability to identify top talent, the confidence to pick smart people, and the capacity to attract talented people to the organization.

- *Identifying Top Talent*: Finding people precisely right for the job requires a knowledge of the organization and its work. It also demands knowledge of self: How will I use this position? Who will be a good match with me? What kind of help will I be needing? A knowledge of the organization's culture is also necessary: Who will be a good fit here? Will this person be happy here?

- *Confidence to Pick Smart People*: This may sound obvious, but it is no trivial requirement. Building optimum organizational brainpower (the ideal goal) demands that leaders be willing to bring aboard people smarter than themselves. It takes confidence to do this—confidence in one's ability to not be intimidated by a superior intellect, and confidence in being able to manage people who know they are smarter than the boss. No mean trick, but necessary. Again, Peter Drucker is instructive: "No executive has ever suffered because his subordinates were strong and effective. There is no prouder boast, but also no better prescription, for executive effectiveness than the words Andrew Carnegie, the father of the U.S. steel industry, chose for his own tombstone: 'Here lies a man who knew how to bring into his service men better than he was himself.'"

- *Capacity to Attract Talented People*: Once they identify the talent, how do leaders draw it to the organization? How do they close the deal? This may be the most difficult task of all. Outstanding people have many options and are attracted to organizations for a variety of reasons: interesting projects, authority, freedom, ideal climate, a leader's personality, and even money. The problem of attracting people is that you normally can't simply ask them what they are seeking. The trick is often to get to know them, build a relationship, and cultivate them until you sense intuitively what will close the deal. Then act on that instinct, perhaps tentatively at first (after all, you're not sure), but move progressively forward until the person joins up. Sound like a lot of trouble? Well, it does take effort, plus time and patience. But getting great people is worth it all.

A final note on retaining good people. After all, getting them is just the first step. Providing development opportunities helps a lot. But empowering them (letting them know you value and trust them) is the magic key to keeping them happy and in the organization. Yet it is surprising how often we fail to empower our people. We may think they already know how we value their abilities, or we may intentionally elect to keep things a little vague. Some leaders feel it's an advantage to keep people a bit off balance—but it is always a mistake. Talented and creative people won't tolerate it. They have other options. So we must provide development opportunities for our good people—and empower them!

When we think about staffing with talent, certain industries come to mind: computer firms, the biotech and pharmaceutical industries, major universities, research hospitals. Without top talent, such enterprises quickly get left behind. The views and actions of some of our presidents can be instructive here as well:

- Theodore Roosevelt said: "Personally, I have never been able to understand why the head of a big business, whether it be the nation, the state, or the Army or Navy should not desire to have very strong and positive people under him."

- Truman biographer, David McCullough, listed some of the distinguished people Truman brought into government, and commented: "The list is long and very impressive. That most of them had more distinguished backgrounds than he, if they were taller, handsomer, it seemed to bother him not at all. When it was suggested to him that General Marshall as Secretary of State might lead people to think Marshall would make a better President, Truman's response was that yes, of course, Marshall would make a better President, but that he, Harry Truman, was President and he wanted the best people possible around him."

- Franklin Roosevelt's selection of wartime military leaders and John Kennedy's cabinet (often referred to as "the best and the brightest") are other examples of hiring top talent.

- George W. Bush is still another useful example. Though we don't know how his presidency will ultimately be regarded, we do know that in Chaney, Powell, Rice, Rumsfeld and others, he was willing to surround himself with people of vastly greater knowledge, experience, and proven abilities than he possessed himself.

The point is: It takes a confident leader to pick a team of very bright people and a very persuasive leader to attract such individuals—but history says a big payoff comes from doing just that.

Your Turn

Do you feel comfortable having people work for you who are smarter than you?

Attend to Management and Institution Building

A word now on management. Top executives with strong personal leadership qualities can still fail, for want of attention to the management of the organization. This doesn't mean total hands-on control. The word "attend" was selected intentionally to convey the need for oversight, awareness, and participation in the establishment of appropriate management systems and policies to implement the strategy:

> To lead you must also manage.

- Structuring for optimum functioning
- Planning processes
- Culture setting
- Information management
- Reward systems
- Communication networks
- Ongoing organizational assessment

> "I try to keep in touch with the details...you've got to have a feel for what's going on."
>
> —Rupert Murdoch

Leaders may delegate the day-to-day management once the design is in place. But they must be key players in the design, and skilled in their essential oversight role. A key aspect of that role is establishing the system of accountability: setting clear standards and performance expectations, ensuring logistical and administrative support, providing feedback on performance, and acting to ensure results. Being a motivator of subordinates and cheerleader in their success is surely important, but the top executive must not ignore the role of critical evaluator of performance.

Management is sometimes considered a knowledge area for the leader—and certainly it is. But it is also a matter of will. Subordinates must know that the boss is conscious of how the system is designed to work, alert to problems, and will be quick to intervene if the ship appears to be drifting off course.

> ### Your Turn
>
> Do you consider management to be a part of leadership, or leadership to be a part of management—or are they the same?

Allocate Resources Effectively

Resource allocation is, of course, a part of management. But it needs to be called out as a specific senior leadership quality. It is the final step in the decision process. In fact, it is often said that decision-making *is* the act of allocating resources.

> Applying resources is the last step in decision-making.

> "There comes a time when you've got to say, 'Let's get off our asses and go'...I have always found that if I move with 75 percent or more of the facts I usually never regret it. It's the guys who wait to have everything perfect that drive you crazy."
>
> —Lee Iacocca

Data are supplied by many, advice by a select brain trust. However, the top executive ultimately must decide: how much money, how many people, which people, which equipment and facilities—to which projects and tasks? The requirement is not for accounting expertise. It is for judgment. Understanding the options, the things competing for resources, the organization's capabilities, the passion of internal proponents, the nature of competition, the external forces, and a sense of opportunity—all play a role in forming that judgment.

The executive can expect a lot of system help on this task, but cannot delegate the responsibility. It is at the heart of the organization's life and strategic direction.

Your Turn

How competent are you in financial and resource allocation matters? What steps could you take to overcome any shortcomings?

Summary

- Senior leaders need unique professional characteristics, such as:
    - A sense of context
    - Perspective
    - Vision
    - Attention to management
    - External orientation
- The characteristics form a framework or lens:
    - To evaluate others
    - To view yourself
    - To aid in self-development
- The lens is the tool; looking with it is the technique.

Chapter 3

Qualities

Objectives

- Recognize senior leadership as a unique role.
- Learn nine personal qualities to evaluate executive qualifications and performance.
- Develop tools to critique senior leaders.
- Develop tools for personal self-development.

This chapter discusses the following nine personal qualities considered essential to senior leader effectiveness:

- Integrity
- Judgment
- Interpersonal and Negotiation skills
- Flexibility
- Tenacity
- Comfort with Ambiguity, Complexity, and Crises
- Nerve and Survival Skills
- High Self-Knowledge/Self-Development Oriented
- Presence/Touch

Integrity

Integrity is the glue that binds people together, and often it is the key to the organization's survival. Examples of the devastating impact of unprincipled or unethical behavior are easy to find. Watergate stands as the primary example in government—so serious it brought down a president. Enron and other firms still under investigation represent equivalent disasters in the private sector. American Catholic bishops, still under fire for their inept handling of sexual abuse cases, provide another illustration of how unprincipled action at the top can shake whole institutions.

Individual breaches within major organizations can be instructive as well. Cases of insider trading come to mind. In some serious cases, lower-level culprits were indeed punished with imprisonment. But what about the people at the top? Though perhaps not prosecutable, is there not a question of ethics here? If you are the boss of someone who is consistently bringing in valuable investment information, isn't there some obligation to ask: Where are you getting your information? The failure to ask the hard questions, to confront individual breaches of ethics and demand accountability, is to neglect one's leadership responsibility. And through such neglect the leader risks his organization, all the people in it, and every stakeholder.

> Integrity is the glue that holds it all together.

> "The supreme quality for a leader is unquestionable integrity. Without it no real success is possible."
>
> —Dwight D. Eisenhower

Personal example is the key. Senior executives need to both have and demonstrate ethical principles in their organizations. Today's world is one of complex networks of interdependent organizations, each operating with a highly mobile workforce and temporary interdepartmental task forces and projects. In such an environment, it is essential for senior executives (themselves highly mobile) to build a reputation for integrity that will follow them to new organizations and be the basis of immediate trust and guidance for all members when those leaders take charge. Achieving this is not easy, but it is necessary. It's not enough to simply profess high moral and ethical principles. Leaders must demonstrate their principles by their actions and, in that way, become role models for others. Further, they must talk about the importance of ethical behavior (to educate the organization), walk the talk, reward those who act on principle, and demand accountability from those who don't. For the goal is not just a principled leader, but a principled organization.

Your Turn

Do you consider integrity the most important leadership quality? Why?

Judgment

Judgment is the ability to make right decisions. Right decisions are those that turn out right in the end. The problem is we can't know how any decision will ultimately turn out. Given that, decision-making becomes a matter of picking courses of action based on "reasonable criteria"—always a leap in the dark. But good judgment permits the leap to be made with more confidence of success. That's what top executives get paid for: their judgment.

Lots of things contribute to judgment. Knowledge of the organization and the interorganizational and global issues is important. The existence of a sound strategy aids judgment. Intuition also plays a part because it helps one jump ahead of all the details and envision possible solutions instinctively. But nothing tells the full story about judgment. It is an almost mystical quality, sometimes called the "mystique of command."

> Judgment is how leaders earn their pay.

> "The principal source of erroneous judgment is viewing things partially and only on one side."
>
> —Samuel Johnson

Getting our arms around the quality of judgment is difficult. An indispensable related skill is a good sense of timing. And in timing considerations, judgment is almost always at war with the activist tendency of many executives. They know that to obtain and hold the support of stakeholders, it is often essential to strike quickly, acting within the window of opportunity. Yet good judgment (setting the right course) often requires suspending action while assembling enough reliable information.

Maybe the most that can be said about judgment is: We know it when we see it. The top executive's record speaks for his or her judgment: a record of mostly right decisions.

Your Turn

Do you consider yourself a person of good judgment? How do you know?

Interpersonal and Negotiation Skills

You never reach a point in the hierarchy where you do not have to deal with people. The top executive's requirement for good interpersonal skills is greater than that of any other member of the organization—for he or she must interact not only with internal members but with all external stakeholders as well.

> "The most important single ingredient in the formula of success is knowing how to get along with people."
>
> —Theodore Roosevelt

People do business with those they like and trust—so good interpersonal skills are needed to attract and retain quality staff and to link the organization to the outside world.

> Negotiation with external constituents is the toughest.

Another factor of concern for senior executives is that most complex problems facing the organization normally demand both internal and external networks for solution. Negotiation with external stakeholders falls predominantly to the top leader, and influencing those outside the organization is always more demanding than dealing with internal people. When leaders are attempting to persuade their own people, a power element always overlays the influence attempt. Power is normally absent when negotiating with external people, so the leader must educate and work especially hard to find common ground.

Your Turn

Think of the most difficult person with whom you must negotiate often. Why is negotiation difficult with this individual? How could you improve the negotiation climate with this person?

Flexibility

The senior leader's job is to match opportunities with capabilities. The starting point, of course, is vision. Vision and the associated strategy can and must provide guidance for decision-making. However, rigid adherence to established vision or strategy can be fatal. Both must be kept under continual review. Circumstances change, but matching opportunity with capabilities remains the constant task—and making that match demands the flexibility to adjust vision and strategy over time.

> Nothing stays constant— nor can you.

> "Whosoever desires constant success must change his conduct with the times."
>
> —Niccolo Machiavelli

The thoughtful leader recognizes that both opportunities and capabilities are moving targets. Attention to the internal management system gives a check on capabilities. Knowledge of the external world helps both in sensing opportunities and acquiring new resources and capabilities. Flexibility is the quality that permits action in changing environments.

Your Turn

If three of your smartest but most difficult subordinates met for lunch and discussed your leadership, would they say you were appropriately flexible? Would they say they wanted more or less flexibility?

Tenacity

Tenacity may seem at war with flexibility—but it really isn't. Flexibility, the ability and willingness to change course, is vital in a changing world. However, tenacity in the pursuit of purpose is equally important.

Sometimes you must hold fast to the task.

So, what is tenacity? It's the strength to face and overcome obstacles and not falter in difficult circumstances, and the ability to ride out

> "Most people give up just when they're about to achieve success. They quit on the one-yard line."
>
> —H. Ross Perot

tactical defeats in pursuit of long-term strategy. Tenacity is another quality that we recognize when we see it.

Tenacity is often first noticed in the tone and content of the leader's statement of purpose and strategy. An outstanding illustration is this passage from Winston Churchill's speech in the House of Commons on May 13, 1940.

> "We have before us an ordeal of the most grievous kind. We have before us many, many long months of struggle and of suffering. You ask, what is our policy? I will say: It is to wage war by sea, land, and air, with all our might and with all the strength that God can give us: to wage war against a monstrous tyranny, never surpassed in the dark, lamentable catalogue of human crime. That is our policy. You ask, what is our aim? I can answer in one word: Victory—victory at all costs, victory in spite of all terror, victory, however long and hard the road may be; for without victory, there is no survival."

Great statement—but words are only a start. Churchill demonstrated tenacity by following through with consistent action through all the years of World War II.

Your Turn

If three of your smartest but most difficult subordinates met for lunch and discussed your leadership, how would they rate you on the quality of tenacity? Would they be correct in their judgment?

Comfort with Ambiguity, Complexity, and Crises

If there is one overarching trend in organizations today, it is the growth in ambiguity and complexity—internally, because of the rapid expansion of knowledge and technology; and externally, because of increasing acquisitions, mergers, and other forms of collaboration. This leads to high levels of uncertainty and interdependence. We all crave certainty when planning and making decisions. But today's thoughtful leader knows that few certainties exist, and to expect a perfect decision environment where all the facts are crystal clear is to invite disappointment, and possibly failure.

However, simply recognizing that the organizational world is complex and ambiguous is not enough. Successful top executives tend to be *comfortable* in this turbulent environment.

> Stay cool—
> especially
> under pressure.

> "Anyone can hold the helm when the sea is calm."
>
> —Publicius Syrus

They are savvy enough to know that demanding certainty of facts and predictions from staff will get them bad recommendations. They know to plan tentatively, and with a degree of humility and respect for the turbulence. They empower subordinates with smart guidance: "Look, let's acknowledge that none of us can predict with certainty what to do. What I want from you is your take on the uncertainties and your best judgment of how to move forward." Such executives avoid the pitfall of letting uncertainty lead to either rash moves or paralysis.

Crises are inevitable in turbulent environments. Things are bound to go wrong. The leader must recognize that people and systems function differently in crisis and that bad news can't be expected to improve without action—the leader's action.

The management of crises is so important to effective senior leadership that Part III of this book focuses exclusively on this skill. A set of principles is provided to guide the leader in crises, and a number of historical examples are used to illustrate the importance of the principles. The point to be made here, however, is that successful top leaders must not only be skilled at preventing and managing crises—they must be *comfortable* in the crisis environment. The very best leaders thrive on the challenge.

We don't need to look far for validation of this idea. Think of past presidents confronted with crises. The ones who seemed to truly enjoy the challenges (FDR, Reagan, Kennedy, Truman) were successful in crises. Those who let a crisis drag them down (e.g., Carter by the Iran hostage crisis; Lyndon Johnson by the Vietnam War) ultimately failed in their leadership.

> ### Your Turn
>
> How comfortable are you in leadership situations characterized by a crisis environment or a high degree of ambiguity or complexity? Would your bosses, subordinates, and peers agree with your assessment?

Nerve and Survival Skills

Much more will be said about nerve later in Part IV, on risk taking. But some mention of it must be made here in this collection of executive qualities. So often in the uncertain decision environment, senior leaders are at the mercy of their instincts. Decision-making becomes a leap in the dark: making a choice from among a number of unclear or marginal alternatives.

But decisions must be made. And, in the most difficult ones, the top executive must stand alone as the responsible party. Doing this takes nerve because the leader knows there is danger from many quarters:

> Never let them get you down.

> "A successful man is one who can lay a firm foundation with the bricks others have thrown at him."
>
> —David Brinkley

- Boards of Directors
- Stockholders
- Peers
- Competitors
- Employees

Any and all stakeholders can become angry and disgruntled when things go wrong, as they often do. It takes nerve to lead in the first place, and good survival skills to stay in the saddle when many are screaming for your head. Successful leaders know: You can't win if you are not around to play. They know how to outlast the opposition.

Your Turn

Have you ever taken a big hit professionally—one that threatened your career? Are you satisfied with the way you reacted? In hindsight, would you make any change in your reaction?

High Self-Knowledge/Self-Development Oriented

This quality is important because it grounds leaders and guides much of their actions. Questions all top executives should ask themselves and be able to answer include:

- What are my strengths and weaknesses?
- What work do I like to do?
- What work do I hate to do?
- Do I learn best by listening or by reading?
- How do I use staff—to present the whole story to me, or to distill information into a concise package?
- How much of what functions am I willing to delegate?

> You have to know yourself before you can lead others.

> "It is the capacity to develop and improve their skills that distinguishes leaders from their followers."
>
> —Warren Bennis and Bert Nanus
> *Leaders*

Without answers to those and similar questions it is impossible for a top executive to design a supporting organizational system and staff it with people who are the right fit. And maybe the most important question (and toughest to face) involves the executive's credibility. That question is: Why would anyone trust that I know what I'm doing? It's an important question because credibility is needed to inspire followers.

Successful executives usually have a good handle on themselves. Those who fail often do not know the answer to the questions posed here, or maybe don't even know enough to ask those questions.

And good self-knowledge pays off because it is usually accompanied by an interest in self-development. Leaders smart enough to spot critical weaknesses are those most motivated to find ways to improve. They are willing to explore the full range of skills for self-management and self-care: time and stress management, creativity enhancement, physical fitness and wellness, an inclination toward lifelong learning, and a sense of balance in work and life.

In summary, the overall result of high self-knowledge is both a true assessment of the role one can play and an enhancement of that role through the increased skill and energy generated by self-development efforts.

Your Turn

What efforts have you made in the past five years to assess your professional strengths and weaknesses or engage in professional self-development activities? Are you satisfied with this level of effort?

Presence/Touch

To be effective, the top leader must be visible. Effective leaders may find different ways to maintain contact with their followers—but they cannot and do not hide, for any reason.

> Leading requires showing up at the right time.

In their popular book, *Primal Leadership: Realizing the Power of Emotional Intelligence*, Daniel Goleman, Richard Boyatzis, and Annie McKee argue that "the fundamental task of leaders is to prime good feeling in those they lead (by creating) resonance—a reservoir of positivity that frees the best in people." Since strong leadership is most necessary in crises and risky situations, it is especially noteworthy that the authors argue "In grave crisis, all eyes turn to the leader for emotional guidance. Because the leader's way of seeing things has special weight, leaders manage meaning for a group, offering a way to interpret or make sense of it, and so react emotionally to a given situation." In sum, they regard the leader's emotions as contagious—capable of driving the emotions of others, and their performance, in

> "I used to say to him that his presence on the field made the difference of forty thousand men."
>
> —Duke of Wellington (about Napoleon)

either a positive or negative direction. This, of course, is true of leaders at every level—but it is particularly important at the most senior levels.

Good leaders touch followers emotionally. You must be present to achieve this touch. And you can't fake it: People can detect a counterfeit in a heartbeat. The message: To play the game you must be there!

<u>Your Turn</u>

In leadership roles, what techniques do you use to maintain "presence" or "emotional contact" with your people?

Summary

- Senior leaders need unique qualities, such as:
  - Integrity
  - Judgment
  - Flexibility
  - Tenacity
  - Nerve and survival skills
- The qualities form a framework or lens:
  - To evaluate others
  - To view yourself
  - To aid in self-development
- The lens is the tool; looking with it is the technique.

Application Exercises

Exercise #1: Senior Leader Characteristics and Qualities

Copy the list of the nineteen characteristics and qualities. Indicate to the left of each the degree to which you feel that characteristic or quality is important to your future: High (H), Moderate (M), or Low (L). Indicate to the right the degree to which you feel you possess that characteristic or quality: High (H), Moderate (M), or Low (L). Next, circle those characteristics that you indicated were highly important to you, but that you possess to only a moderate or low degree. Finally, list some actions you might take to improve in those areas where you have shortcomings.

Thoughts on the Exercise

- Some characteristics lend themselves well to self-study or picking the brains of others (e.g., understanding the work of the organization, communicating effectively, and allocating resources).

- In some areas, improvement can be achieved simply by raising one's consciousness of the importance of the issue (e.g., sense of context, perspective, strategic thinking).

- With some qualities (e.g., flexibility, tenacity, nerve), it may be sufficient just to keep in mind the importance of the item as one struggles to lead.

- A quality like judgment could call for specific actions, such as consulting widely and taking more time in decision-making.

Exercise #2: Executive Perspective

Copy the list of role differences between top executives and lower-level managers. Examine each pair of statements and circle those where your tendency is to have the lower management rather than the executive perspective. Now ask yourself two questions: If placed in an executive position, would you have difficulty shifting your perspective in those circled roles? What could you do by way of self-development to have better command of any executive roles where you have weaknesses?

Thoughts on the Exercise

The major value of this list of role differences is to make you conscious that a major change in perspective is necessary as one reaches the top. All the top executive roles listed are important to performance. Some of them might require new learning. For example, some excellent processes are available to assist in studying the environment and in setting goals. But you can master most of the executive roles simply by recognizing the need and willing yourself to behave in accordance with the roles.

Part II

Ability to Manage Change

"There is nothing permanent except change."

—Heraclitus

The purpose of this module is to help the reader design and manage organizational change efforts—an essential senior leadership skill.

To lead is to move the organization forward—and that means change. The change can take many forms:

- New leadership
- New products or services
- New technology
- Redesigned tasks or jobs
- New markets
- Internationalization
- Culture change (e.g., to faster pace; to greater customer service orientation)

The list of possible changes is long. But two things are certain: Change can't be avoided if progress is to be made, and change is never easy. Niccolo Machiavelli made the point well, 500 years ago:

> "There is nothing more difficult to carry out, nor more doubtful of success, nor more dangerous to handle than to initiate a new order of things. For the reformer has enemies in all who profit by the old order, and only lukewarm defenders by all those who could profit by the new order. This lukewarmness arises from the incredulity of mankind who do not truly believe in anything new until they have had actual experience with it."

The literature on change emphasizes the leader's role in *creating* change—and this is indeed an important role. *Change creation* is a part of the development of the organization's strategy. A leader can certainly fail for lack of imagination in this role. But more often, failure occurs through a lack of attention to *managing the change process*: Hence the emphasis in this module is on *managing change*.

The concepts in this module are derived from considerable personal experience with change efforts as a participant or consultant. Thus, much of it is written in the first person and is somewhat autobiographical.

I began studying change twenty-five years ago in a doctoral dissertation. That research produced a theory for managing change that has since been tested and refined through numerous consulting engagements. Those experiences with change have led to a conviction that four facts are always true about change and four mistakes are almost always made by leaders of change.

Four Facts

- Many people will resist any change.

- Some will value the status quo no matter how bad it is.

- Some will fear for their future in the changed situation.

- Regardless of the leader's credentials, many people will not trust that the leader knows what he or she is doing when proposing change.

Four Mistakes

- Failing to get personally involved.

- Going too fast.

- Promising too much to those above and to those below. Leaders promise too much to those above to gain permission for change; they promise too much to those below to get people to accept the change.

- Failing to communicate—early, fully, consistently, and continually—throughout the process. Lack of information breeds rumor, anger, and anxiety—thus heightening opposition.

This module provides a set of nine principles for managing change. As a vehicle for validating the principles, four actual cases of organizational change are used. They are all cases in which I was personally involved as either a participant or consultant.

The four cases are described first. These case narratives, even without benefit of change management principles, are instructive. They alert one to the variety and pervasiveness of change. After the discussion of all four cases, the nine principles for managing change are discussed and validated through references to appropriate cases.

The material is divided into two chapters:

- Chapter 4   Change Cases
- Chapter 5   Principles for Managing Change

As in Part I, each chapter begins with learning objectives and ends with summary points. At the end of the discussion of each principle a "Your Turn" question is posed to help you reflect on the material and relate it to your experience.

In summary, Part II is a comprehensive learning module on change. Its objectives are to sharpen the lens with which you view organizational change situations and provide specific principles to guide your actions in designing and implementing a new organizational change or in drawing lessons learned from past change efforts.

The best way to navigate this module is to first read the module's introductory material, which discusses the importance of change management, and then read Chapter 4, which describes four actual change cases. With these four cases in mind, read Chapter 5, which states nine principles for managing change and illustrates them by referring to the cases in Chapter 4. As you read, stop briefly to reflect on the many "Your Turn" questions. Next, review the chapter objectives and summaries. And, finally, complete the application exercises.

What result should you expect? Not simply memory of the principles—you'll always have access to them. Rather, you should sense a greater awareness of change situations and an improved confidence in your ability to use the principles to better design, implement, or critique an organizational change.

Chapter 4

Change Cases

Objectives

- Recognize the nature, prevalence, and impact of organizational change.
- Learn the details of four true cases of change.
- Recognize the need to facilitate change.
- Understand the role of the senior leader in the change process.

This chapter discusses the following four cases of organizational change:

- U.S. Army War College—Curriculum change
- Manufacturing Plant—Change of equipment and job descriptions
- College MBA Program—Change to an accelerated program
- County Government—Change of equipment and procedures

These are all true cases in which I played some role. They include examples of both successful and unsuccessful change management—in business, government, and non-profit organizations.

The cases immerse the reader in the change environment and highlight the impact of change in organizations and the critical role of the leader in change management. The good and bad examples of change management found in this set of cases are then used in the next chapter to validate the nine principles for managing change.

Case #1:   U S. Army War College-Curriculum Change

My involvement in this change was as the primary participant and proponent for the change.

In 1977, I was an army colonel newly assigned to the U.S. Army War College as Chair of the Command, Leadership, and Management Department. The War College provided a nine-month graduate-level education program for 250 competitively selected lieutenant colonels with about eighteen years of service. The three main areas of study were: leadership and management, military

> In proposing change, expect resistance. Don't assume that others will trust your judgment. Legitimate!!!

> "If change is to occur, it must come about through hard work within the organization itself."
>
> —Gordon Lippitt

strategy, and domestic and international relations. My department had responsibility for designing and presenting the leadership and management portion of the curriculum. I had fifteen faculty members in the department—all army colonels with command experience. Each had an additional management specialty area (e.g., personnel, research and development, logistics, financial management, training, organizational development).

The method for delivering instruction was unusual. Students were divided into fifteen sections. Each faculty member was assigned to a section and taught all the subject matter to that section. If the day's topic was financial management, the faculty member most expert in that area prepared a comprehensive instructional packet for that day and pre-briefed other faculty members on the packet until all felt comfortable presenting the material to their sections and guiding discussion. This process was followed for all topics in the curriculum. This instructional method may seem odd, but it was long-term school policy. It could not be changed by me.

The overall program was demanding. Each department felt it needed more curriculum time to present its material. Also, within my department, the various subject experts were alert to any proposal that might lessen the time devoted to their specialty area.

At the time I became chair, I was in the middle of a doctoral program that had a strong behavioral component using a battery of self-assessment instruments to assist students in recognizing their styles of leadership and identifying strengths and weaknesses. Emphasis was placed on developing an enhanced style range: more ways to lead, motivate, handle conflict, etc.

I felt that I had been helped significantly by this self-assessment process. The Army War College had nothing in this area for its students. I wanted to introduce a similar program, taught by my department faculty. Thus, a change effort was born!

I arrived at the start of an academic year—and decided to launch a year-long campaign to introduce this new program in the next academic year. I estimated the new material would require about five days of instructional time. I also decided that I would make this change effort the subject of my doctoral dissertation. The dissertation design had three elements: first, a literature search to develop a tentative list of principles to manage change; second, use of those principles to begin to facilitate the change; and finally, revision of the principles based on what the experience taught me about change.

Space here is not sufficient to tell this whole story. But some of the problems and issues faced were as follows:

- Convincing the Commandant (head of the College) that this was a worthwhile idea.

- Convincing my department faculty that the idea had merit, and dealing with the permanently unconvinced.

- Bargaining for curriculum time: There were strong proponents for other instruction, in and out of the department.

- Training the faculty to administer the program. Many were uncomfortable with experiential learning processes but, under our system, all would have to teach it.

- Selling the idea to students, many of whom were skeptical of the value of this type of training.

The bottom line is that the program was introduced the next year and was very well received by the students. But it was a struggle to get it going, and the process was a great learning experience on facilitating change.

Case #2:   Manufacturing Plant—Change of Equipment and Job Descriptions

My involvement in this change was as a consultant to the plant manager. I was asked for advice after the change process was underway because employees were upset about the change.

This plant of 500 employees was part of a large corporation that manufactured food products. The plant manager was attempting to boost productivity by installing new equipment in the final stage of the production line and

> An early, complete, and uniform presentation of a change idea is important to acceptance.

redesigning and reclassifying the jobs of the 150 employees working there.

I became involved in mid-October. The change was already underway, and the plant manager wanted to have the new system up and running in January. Employees were nerv-

> "Even in slight things the experience of the new is rarely without some stirring of foreboding."
>
> —Eric Hoffer

ous about the change, fearful for their jobs, and resisting the rapid move to the new system. I had been involved with the plant for several years, knew the people well, and was asked to assess the situation and make recommendations.

This situation had many of the ingredients of the most volatile and disruptive kind of change, for the following reasons:

- It was a very big change in terms of the number of people involved (over 150 people). That was almost a third of the total plant employees. So, if it didn't go well, it would be a very big problem, just because of the large number of people impacted by the change.

- It meant *system change* for many: They would move to a merit pay system by virtue of reclassification.

- It introduced a competitive requirement that would require people to learn new skills or suffer status and salary penalties.

- It would result in work climate changes: The proposal moved people from known tasks to unknown, from simple to more complex tasks, and toward an atmosphere of less comfort and security than they currently enjoyed.

- Even though some people would emerge with better pay, more status, and enriched jobs as a result of the change, people could not be certain (at the start) of the outcome implications for themselves. Many naturally were worried about their positions in the organization.

- This change crossed departmental lines. It would eventually have implications beyond the production-line employees, and impact also sanitation and maintenance positions. This fact served to arouse concerns in many people not involved in the initial reorganization activities.

My suggestions to the plant manager included:

- Slow down the process.

- Develop a good briefing, and make sure every employee hears it quickly to counter rumors and reduce anxiety.

- Stress (in the briefing) the protections that will be part of the plan: Training can be repeated until mastered. No one will lose their job. No one will get less pay as a result of reclassification.

- Pilot-test the briefing with a small group of bright people and refine it before it goes to everyone.

- After hearing the briefing, have employees submit any concerns anonymously, and respond to those.

- Set up a system for updating people on status at frequent intervals.

- Be careful what you promise to people outside the plant on this. You don't know for sure how to quantize the benefits, so don't put yourself in a box with Corporate Headquarters. Be modest and tentative about your expectations.

This was actually a very useful change for this plant. Once employees were fully informed, most saw the benefits for the plant and for themselves. Redesigning the change plan did cause the completion date to slip several months but, once in place, employees viewed it favorably and production did improve.

Case #3:   College MBA Program—Change to an Accelerated Program

I was on the receiving end of this change. I was a member of the business faculty in my college when the administration began considering the idea of trying to boost MBA program enrollments by changing the program from a traditional (semester) structure to a more accelerated format.

At the time, our college had 1400 undergraduate students, of whom 400 were business, economics, or accounting majors. We also had an evening MBA program serving about 300 part-time students. The same faculty (fifteen full-time, plus some part-time) served both programs.

For several years, we had been experiencing increasing competition for MBA students, resulting in declining enrollments. Our program had always been taught in a traditional semester format: Courses met for fifteen weeks, one night per week, for two and a half

> To facilitate change, you must involve all interested parties.

> "Force has no place where there is need of skill."
>
> —Herodotus

hours. We were losing students to other institutions that were offering courses in a more accelerated mode: fewer, but longer class meetings; courses completed in about eight weeks.

One large national university began offering consulting services to smaller institutions desiring to move to accelerated programs. Our college administration had them brief our department faculty on their approach. Our business faculty did not like these people and hoped the "acceleration" idea would go away and not be considered further for our MBA program. But—it was not to be so.

The college leadership was rightly dissatisfied with our declining MBA enrollments and asked us repeatedly for recommendations to improve things. Unhappy with our response (which was indeed weak), they began to think seriously about accelerating the program. Their exact intentions were not clear, but it appeared to us that they were considering three possibilities: Have two programs (one traditional and one accelerated), force us to develop a single accelerated program, or turn things over to the consulting group. The faculty's uncertainty about these intentions caused much anxiety. We disagreed with the change and also feared having our program run by an outside group that we did not like or respect. I'm not saying outside management was the administration's intention (I really don't know)—but that was our perception of the most likely outcome.

The concerns of our faculty about accelerating were many: Would the students like this new format (fewer meetings, longer meetings, more homework)? Could courses that were being taught in fifteen weeks be compressed and still retain appropriate coverage of material? Were all our faculty capable of teaching in this new mode? What would be the role of the consulting group in program design and faculty hiring and assessment?

To make a long story short: We voluntarily redesigned our MBA program (to six, seven-week sessions per year). We got agreement from the administration that we would not need to deal with the consulting group—that it would be totally *our* program. We ate our technical concerns in the interest of keeping control of the program.

The change? Oh yes, it was the right thing to do. Students liked it, faculty proved competent to deliver it, and enrollment significantly increased. But there is a lesson here: Change does not come easily. It takes skill and effort to achieve smooth implementation.

Case #4:   County Government—Change of Equipment and Procedures

My involvement in this change was as consultant to the county government. As in the case of the manufacturing plant, I was asked for advice during the change implementation because employees were upset.

> In assessing a change, people worry first about themselves.

The county had purchased new software that would change a multitude of county processes: hiring, paying county employees, registering students at the community college, record keeping, etc. The county negotiated a service contract with the IBM Corporation to get the system operating and train the people.

> "Man acts from motives relative to his interests; and not from metaphysical speculations."
>
> —Edmund Burke

Initially, no one was sufficiently sensitive to employee concerns about this change: How is my job going to change? Is this better than what we have? Is it better for me? Can I master the new technology? However, the personnel department was run by a very savvy manager with lots of experience. He quickly saw a problem was brewing and decided to take action. His prompt intervention prevented this from becoming a huge problem and greatly facilitated the change process. Here's what was done:

- A mailing was sent to all involved employees (about 100 people) that clearly explained the change project and asked them to provide (anonymously) a list of their concerns.

- All employees were required to attend a meeting at which each submitted concern was addressed. IBM consultants responded on all technical issues and county managers addressed administrative matters.

- After all submitted questions were covered, employees worked in small groups to identify any remaining issues, which were then addressed in the meeting.

- Attendees were informed that a newsletter would be provided at regular intervals to update them on the project, and that periodic meetings also would be held to provide an opportunity for discussion of future concerns.

This change went well. People initially had a lot of anxiety about the change, but they quickly settled down once they had received full information, had their specific questions answered, and saw a system in place to keep them updated. This is an example of a management alert to change problems.

Summary

- Change is a permanent phenomenon.
- Leaders always bring change.
- People normally fear and resist change.
- Facilitating change:
    - Is necessary and possible
    - Requires early recognition
    - Demands deep leader involvement
    - Calls for deliberate intervention strategies

Chapter 5

Principles for Managing Change

Objectives

- Recognize the need for a deliberate strategy or tool to facilitate change.
- Understand nine principles useful in facilitating change.
- Learn to use the principles as a tool for change management.

This chapter discusses the following nine principles for managing change:

- Be alert: Recognize when you are involved with change.
- Get personally involved immediately, and stay engaged.
- Think conceptually: Use theory to guide the change.
- Consider forces and trends for and against you.
- Consider the organization's culture.
- Validate the change idea.
- Develop a clear presentation explaining the change.
- Build evaluation into the change plan: Get early and continuous feed-back on progress.
- Manage the dynamics of the change process.

Each principle is stated in the form of an action step, then discussed briefly and validated by one or more of the four cases presented in Chapter 4. The set of principles represents a framework or lens to view change—and a tool for the leader to effectively manage change.

1. *Be alert: Recognize when you are involved with change.*

Many of the actions contemplated by leaders—maybe most actions—represent change to some people in their organization. It's fine to focus hard on new objectives. But leaders also need to know when ideas they're pushing represent change. Many top leaders come late to the realization that they are dealing with change. This always leads to trouble. All the four case examples are instructive on this point:

You can't deal with change until you recognize it.	- At the Army War College, I knew from the start that others would strongly resist the change. Yet, even though deliberate efforts were made to facilitate the change, many difficulties were experienced. Had I blundered into it, and neglected to plan the change process, it would have undoubtedly failed.	"If you want to truly understand something, try to change it." —Kurt Lewin

- The manufacturing plant and MBA cases show what can happen when leaders, even with good ideas, neglect the change process and move too far without carrying the organization with them.

- In the county example, trouble was avoided by alert management, sensitive to change and acting quickly.

> ### Your Turn
>
> Do you think it is possible for a leader to advocate change, yet not recognize that some organizational members will be threatened by it?

2. *Get personally involved immediately—and stay engaged.*

Boss involvement is essential for successful change.	Change facilitation is tough to do—impossible without the steady hand of the person at the top, not just at the start, but throughout implementation:	"Genius is one percent inspiration and 99 percent perspiration." —Thomas Edison

- In the Army War College case, I was the change proponent. But I sought approval from the Commandant (top leader) before starting and kept him in the loop throughout the process. There was never a doubt among the participants that the top leader supported the change and was following its progress. Support from department faculty was skimpy initially. Without support from the very top, the idea would likely have floundered and ultimately failed.

- In the manufacturing plant case, the plant manager was very involved in the development of the change idea but trusted his subordinate managers with implementation. They were excellent people but not change-sensitive. The difficulties arose because the top leader took his hands off the controls for too long. Had he remained engaged, he surely would have sensed trouble earlier.

- The county government action to promise frequent updates by newsletter and to hold periodic meetings to discuss problem areas is a good example of staying engaged. And it worked!

Your Turn

Once having set the course for change, do you think it is ever appropriate for the leader to delegate responsibility for implementation, then move on personally to other concerns?

---

3. *Think conceptually: Use theory to guide the change.*

There is a lot of good change theory (some here, hopefully). Thinking conceptually is the opposite of "winging it"—it is using theory to guide action:

- At the Army War College, change theory was used to move the idea forward. Making this project into a doctoral dissertation forced me to proceed with change theory in mind. That theory made life as a change proponent a lot easier.

Sound theory helps in planning change.

- As consultant in both the manufacturing plant and county government projects, I discussed change management principles with the organizations and then used those

"Chance favors only the prepared mind."

—Louis Pasteur

principles to recommend action. As always, theory helped. We could not have moved forward without theory to guide us.

Your Turn

Do you think it is possible to be a successful proponent of change without theory to guide your actions?

---

4. *Consider forces and trends—for and against you.*

Leaders, enthusiastic about their ideas, often underestimate the forces opposing them—a bad mistake illustrated in all four cases. Likewise, failure to focus on favorable trends can blind leaders to opportunities for support:

> Bucking forces and trends makes change tough.

- In the MBA case, the forces favoring program acceleration were strong: Many other colleges and universities nationally and regionally had done it, and their enrollments had significantly improved. The administration knew these trends, but did not make the case in a credible way. By having this information briefed by an inept consulting group, they pretty much guaranteed that the information would not be

> "Systems thinking shows us that there is no outside; that you and the cause of your problems are part of a single system."
>
> —Peter Senge

accepted. Had senior administration officials personally brought the same information to the business faculty, they might have more easily gotten the support needed to move forward.

- Likewise, the county government could have used many examples of other organizations successfully transitioning to the same software system with resulting productivity improvements. But they did not capitalize on this trend.

> ### Your Turn
>
> Think of some change you would like to advocate in your organization. What are the forces for and against that change?

5. *Consider the organization's culture.*

A key question confronting every change proponent is: How much authority do I have to require change, and how much effort must I apply to educate and persuade participants? The organization's culture is a key factor in the decision: Do you pick the lock, or break down the door—on the way to change?

> Culture often dictates the change strategy.

- Conventional thinking might say the army culture would permit a leader to act unilaterally with full authority. And, in many circumstances, it does. But the culture at the Army War College was very collegial. Consequently, it was necessary to rely largely on education and persuasion to advance the change there. Though ultimately I did direct that it be done, I had first marshaled a lot of support through education.

> "We had to change major habits in our culture."
>
> —Lee Iacocca (on Chrysler Corporation)

- The civilian college culture is always collegial. Thus, the MBA change needed to be accomplished through extensive education and consultation, taking into account faculty concerns. Failure to do this early enough caused problems.

- The county government, like any bureaucracy, could dictate direction—and initially did. But that didn't eliminate the need to consider participants' feelings. Progress was at a standstill until those feelings were surfaced and addressed. Bureaucracy today is not what it was decades ago. People want a voice.

> ### Your Turn
>
> Describe the culture of your present organization. How might that culture impact the design and implementation of change?

6. *Validate the change idea.*

Knowing what you are doing should perhaps be enough to convince others—but it rarely is. Leaders of change must recognize that others are unlikely to trust their wisdom. They must get outside expert opinion and search for success stories elsewhere to validate or legitimate their ideas:

Outside expert opinion helps convince others.	"No man ever quite believes in any other man." —H.L. Mencken

-   The county government was not the first organization or county to adopt the new information system, and there were dozens of stories of college MBA programs successfully moving to accelerated formats. However, neither organization used this information as effectively as it should have to legitimate its change effort.

-   The changes suggested at the Army War College were already operative in executive programs all over the country. However, the faculty members were unwilling to accept the idea until this evidence was brought to their attention.

> ### Your Turn
>
> Do you think it is always necessary for a leader to take deliberate steps to validate the need for a proposed change?

7. *Develop a clear presentation explaining the change.*

A clear, comprehensive, and consistent message is essential. It should include validation findings (as proof of a sound idea), show respect for the status quo, identify areas of continuity with the past, and point out the advantages for the organization and each individual. It must be careful to not over-sell and candid about risks.

As part of the development of a presentation, it is wise to progressively expose it to criticism from trusted peers, bosses, and key opinion formers. It should be pilot tested and revised as necessary before rolling it out to the whole organization. But testing and revision must be done quickly to stay ahead of the power curve. Rumors spread fast and can contaminate the process.

> Your presentation must sell your change case.

> "The leader must know, must know that he knows, and must be able to make it abundantly clear to those about him that he knows."
>
> —Clarence B. Randall

In all the cases discussed here, and in every other change effort I've observed, no progress was made without a solid presentation. In most problem cases, it was the lack of a presentation that caused much of the initial opposition.

> ### Your Turn
>
> Does your experience confirm the importance of a clear presentation in implementing change?

8. *Build evaluation into the change plan: Get early and continuous feedback on progress.*

Feedback needs to start at the end of the initial briefing: What are your questions? Your ideas? Your concerns? Those questions need to be asked throughout the process, at frequent intervals. It not only reduces resistance, but it permits the leader to use the resistance to sharpen ideas during the process:

> Evaluation and feedback keep change on course.

> "In a time of drastic change, it is the learners who inherit the future."
>
> —Eric Hoffer

- The county government responded to employee concerns by revising its system for managing the change. A good orientation briefing (finally), discussion after that briefing, newsletter updates, and subsequent periodic meetings and discussions were important ingredients for success. There were also elements of evaluation in that revised process—but the evaluation system needs to be in place from the start.

- In both the Army War College and MBA cases, extensive feedback was taken from students and faculty as the change was implemented and after programs were in place. Results were studied and actions taken to tune up the changed programs.

Your Turn

Why is it important to build the system for evaluation and feedback into the original design of a change effort?

---

9. *Manage the dynamics of the change process.*

It's not enough to simply check the status of things. A leader proposing change needs a mindset that says: I'm going into uncharted and uncertain waters. Things will go wrong, and I need to learn as I go and act to adjust plans accordingly. But senior leaders are typically an impatient lot. When they get a new idea, they want implementation to occur soonest. Eager subordinates develop schedules, budgets, and timetables to please the top. People down below worry about the future, though they rarely (due to poor or late orientation) understand it. But they do sense the momentum; they can feel its impact in their daily routine—and it scares them. Anxious and stressed, they resist the change. And leaders are often the last to know why suddenly everything seems to be going wrong.

> Things will go wrong. Keep your hands on the controls.

> "All progress is precarious, and the solution of one problem brings us face to face with another problem."
>
> —Martin Luther King, Jr.

Think back to our four cases, particularly the manufacturing plant and county government examples. Problems developed because leaders were late in recognizing that the change was not understood and that the pace was too fast. The solution? Use the evaluation plan (Principle #8) to furnish data to an overall learning system. And use that learning to drive action: new goals, adjusted timetables, better orientation or training—whatever is necessary to move forward successfully.

Your Turn

Why should we expect any change effort to be unpredictable?

There you have it: my best prescription—a sort of cookbook for managing change. But to be honest with you, this set of principles is offered with much humility and a note of caution. Change is tough, no question about it. Beyond the issue of whether the change is good (i.e., is it sound strategy?), there are lots of things to worry about. Here are a half dozen of them:

- *Timing—in the life of the organization*: Is the change right for us *now*?

- *Support—from the top*: You can't expect to get far with an idea unless you have at least tacit approval from "your boss" (and even the CEO has a boss).

- *Timetable*: Is the pace too fast? Will slowing it down make a big difference in gaining acceptance? Should you consider some pilot testing or schedule changes?

- *Credibility and power*: How much do you have and how much will you need? And, importantly, how will you fill the gaps?

- *Multiple impacts and unintended consequences*: Pushing major change can be likened to unleashing a tiger in a park: You can't predict where it will go or what it will do—but you can predict it will cause problems. Have you considered what elements of the organization might be affected in unexpected and unintended ways? Have you prepared for such contingencies?

- *Institutionalization of the change*: You've designed a good change—good for the organization and the people in it. And you've skillfully planned for and implemented the change. But an important question remains: Will the change endure your departure (for, sooner or later, you will leave)? It makes little sense to bring about change without appropriate attention to the long-term institutionalization of the change. It is not easy, but it can be done. It usually involves arranging some strong proponents for the change within the chain of command. And, you have to plan for this—it is unlikely to happen by accident.

Summary

- Change:
    - Is always underway in organizations
    - Is never easy to achieve
    - Must and can be facilitated
- Certain principles help, such as:
    - Be alert: Recognize when you are involved with change.
    - Consider forces and trends for and against you.
    - Develop a clear presentation explaining the change.
    - Build evaluation into the change plan.
    - Manage the dynamics of the change process.
- The principles form a framework or lens to view change and manage it.
- The lens is the tool; using it to guide action is the technique.

Application Exercises

Exercise #1: Using Principles to Plan Change

Think of some change you would like to see implemented in your organization or some other organization. Then, assume you are responsible for planning the change. Briefly describe the situation. Then, using the principles below as a guide, state the actions you would take to facilitate the change.

1. Be alert: Recognize when you are involved with change.
2. Get personally involved immediately, and stay engaged.
3. Think conceptually: Use theory to guide the change.
4. Consider forces and trends for and against you.
5. Consider the organization's culture.
6. Validate the change idea.
7. Develop a clear presentation explaining the change.
8. Build evaluation into the change plan: Get early and continuous feedback on progress.
9. Manage the dynamics of the change process.

Thoughts on the Exercise

- Theory is useful to guide actions—and the nine principles of change can be considered a comprehensive theory for planning change.

- This exercise gives you an opportunity to use this theory to plan a change of your choice.

- One caution: Do not be content with simply stating a principle as an action (e.g., consider forces and trends for and against you), but try to actually identify detailed actions under the principle (e.g., exactly what are the forces and trends and what you will do about each).

Exercise #2: Using Principles to Critique a Change Effort

Think of some change you have seen implemented in some organization with which you are acquainted. Then, using the change principles from the previous exercise as a guide, critique the way the organization planned and implemented the change.

Thoughts on the Exercise

- Theory can be useful in critiquing an event that has already taken place, and thus learning from the experience.
- The nine principles can be considered as a theory to do such a critique.
- This exercise gives you the opportunity to use this theory to critique a change management situation you have observed.
- As you do the exercise, be sure to consider each and every principle in making your assessment. If you can think of appropriate actions that were not taken, it will tell you that shortcomings occurred in the change management process.

Part III

Ability to Manage Crises

"Competing pressures tempt one to believe that an issue
deferred is a problem avoided: More often it is a crisis invited."

—Henry Kissinger

This module is designed to help the reader deal with crisis situations—to prevent them if possible, to manage them when they occur.

Crises are inevitable in organizational life. They threaten the organization's mission and sometimes even its survival. And leadership is never more important than in times of trouble.

Examine any crisis in history and you find the top leader to be the central figure in the outcome. Crises test leaders, and many fail the test. The purpose here is to develop a set of principles to guide leaders in avoiding and coping with crises. History is the best source for principles—and in this module, six cases will be examined. The specific cases were chosen with the need for balance in mind: Three are corporate, two are government, and one is non-profit. Two are long-past and four are recent and on-going. Three were handled very well and three quite poorly. Collectively, they provide a rich source from which to draw crisis management principles.

The approach here is to first describe all six cases, ending each with some brief comments on the quality of crisis management and a few of the dominant lessons learned. Then a set of principles for crisis management is identified, explained, and validated through references to one or more of the cases or to some very well known incident in history. These crisis cases are summarized as succinctly as possible. Some require more detail than others. But, for each, just enough background is provided to enable the reader to understand the linkage, made later, of cases to principles.

Following the discussion of cases, twenty-six principles are identified and stated as action steps—six to prevent or prepare for crises and twenty to guide action during crises. Each principle is validated through references to appropriate cases.

The material is divided into two chapters:

- Chapter 6   Crises Cases
- Chapter 7   Principles for Managing Crises

Each chapter begins with learning objectives and ends with summary points. And again, many "Your Turn" questions are posed to help you reflect on the material.

In summary, Part III is a comprehensive learning module on crisis management. Its objectives are to sharpen the lens with which you view crises and provide you specific principles to guide your actions in avoiding and managing crises and in drawing lessons learned from past crisis situations.

The best way to navigate this module is to first read the module's introductory material, which discusses the importance of crisis management, and then read Chapter 6, which describes the six historical cases of crisis management. With these six cases in mind, read Chapter 7, which states the twenty-six principles for managing crises and illustrates them by referring to the cases in Chapter 6. As you read, stop briefly to reflect on the many "Your Turn" questions. Next, review the chapter objectives and summaries. And, finally, complete the application exercises.

What result should you expect? Not just memory of the principles—you'll always have access to them. Rather, after completing the reading and exercise material, you should sense a greater awareness of crisis situations and improved confidence in your ability to use the principles to design actions to prevent and manage crises.

Chapter 6

Crisis Cases

Objectives

- Recognize the nature, prevalence, and impact of organizational crises.
- Learn the details of six historical examples of organizational crises.
- Recognize the need for action to prevent and manage crises.
- Understand the role of the senior leader in managing crises.

This chapter discusses the following six historical cases of crisis management.

- Johnson & Johnson's Tylenol Crisis (1982)
- Corporate Malfeasance Crisis: The Business Scandals of 2002
- U2 Spy Plane Crisis (1960)
- Cuban Missile Crisis (1962)
- Memogate: The Crisis at CBS (September 2004)
- Catholic Church Sexual Abuse Crisis (2001–2002)

The set of cases includes examples of both successful and unsuccessful crisis management—in business, government, and non-profit organizations.

The cases immerse the reader in the crisis environment, show the impact of crises, and highlight the essential role of the leader in crisis management. Further, the good and bad examples of crisis management in this set of cases are used in the next chapter to validate the twenty-six principles for managing crises.

Johnson & Johnson's Tylenol Crisis

This is the story of a crisis well handled by one of the country's most respected companies: Johnson & Johnson. The essence of the story is as follows:

In the fall of 1982, seven people died suddenly and in quick succession after taking Tylenol capsules. The company reacted quickly and in accordance

Look first to your values in any crisis.

"The man who is prepared has his battle half-fought."

—Miguel DeCervantes

with its credo:

> We believe our first responsibility is to the doctors, nurses, and patients, to mothers and fathers and all others who use our products and services. In meeting their needs, everything we do must be of high quality.

By sticking to its values, Johnson & Johnson reacted properly and emerged from the crisis with its reputation unscarred by this tragedy.

In the telling of this story, I am deeply indebted to Ronald Houseal, a graduate of the MBA program at Mt. St. Mary's College in Maryland. In 2001, I had the opportunity to serve as his faculty advisor on his master's thesis: *The Tylenol Scare: Did Johnson & Johnson Do The Right Thing?* In the course of his investigation, Ron did extensive research into the literature of this well-documented case, plus he received assistance from the firm. With his permission, I have used the facts he uncovered to prepare this brief summary of the case.

The key events of the case were as follows:

- Wednesday, September 29 Mary Kellerman, a 12-year-old girl in Illinois died in the hospital several hours after taking an extra-strength Tylenol capsule for a cold.

- Just two hours after Kellerman's death (and only a few miles away), Adam Janus went into a coma minutes after taking a Tylenol capsule for shoulder pain. He died shortly thereafter.

- Janus' brother and sister-in-law left the hospital after he died, only to return a few hours later, poisoned by capsules from the same bottle. They also died. Doctors did blood tests, which revealed high levels of cyanide.

- At about the same time, Tylenol capsules from the Kellerman home were tested. These capsules, from the same lot number as Janus' bottle, also tested positive for cyanide.

- These findings of cyanide contamination alerted public health officials to the fact that a serious health emergency had erupted in the Chicago area. Johnson & Johnson officials were notified and took the following actions:

  - Immediately recalled 93,500 bottles of the contaminated lot number (a batch produced in a Pennsylvania plant and shipped to 31 states in the East and Midwest).

  - Dispatched over half a million mailgrams alerting doctors, hospitals, and wholesalers.

- The same day, Mary McFarland, also in the Chicago area, died of tainted capsules from a different lot number (produced in a Texas plant and shipped to Chicago).

- By Friday, 48 hours after the first death, Johnson & Johnson recalled 171,000 bottles with the second lot number.

- An analysis of all the facts, including the chemistry of cyanide, led authorities to conclude that the contamination had occurred in the Chicago area. So, a full court press was done there to warn the public: police bulletins, Boy Scouts going door-to-door, TV, radio, and telephone campaigns. But it was not enough—two more victims died on September 30 and October 2.

Throughout the period of the crisis, Johnson & Johnson acted in a most responsible manner. It continued its all-out effort in behalf of public safety: 22 million bottles of Tylenol were pulled from retailer's shelves (several more tainted bottles were found). Production of the drug was halted. In addition to its own intensive investigation, the firm offered complete cooperation to federal and local authorities and the news media. Further, it offered a $100,000 reward for information on the offenders.

The company was certainly conscious of its public image: It took all those actions plus offered to exchange Tylenol capsules for tablets. In the end, the FDA investigation cleared the company of any involvement in the contamination.

In sum, this was a model of effective crisis management. It is also a story that illustrates how an organization that properly confronts a serious crisis can emerge with its reputation intact, or even (as in this case) enhanced. The key elements of the strategy that successfully led Johnson & Johnson through the crisis were: (1) They recognized the gravity of the situation immediately, (2) they had a very socially responsible credo and used it to guide their actions, (3) they were immediately and completely candid in their public statements and fully cooperated with the authorities, and (4) they did not hesitate to make decisions with significant financial consequences in order to meet their obligation to customers. The result: They landed on their feet, alive and well!

Your Turn

Do you think most U.S. companies would act as responsibly as Johnson & Johnson if faced with a similar crisis?

Corporate Malfeasance:
The Business Scandals of 2002

One thing is certain: The year 2002 will go down in business history as the year corporate malfeasance became most visible in the United States. Misdeeds certainly started a lot earlier, but the extent of malfeasance began to surface and blossomed into a serious crisis in 2002.

Sparking the crisis was the revelation of unethical and in many cases illegal management practices in a number of high-profile firms, including Enron, Arthur Anderson, WorldCom, and Merrill Lynch. The list of firms and transgressions seemed endless, growing all year long. It was a crisis for many reasons: Firms filed for bankruptcy, thousands lost their jobs, retirement funds evaporated, and investors watched portfolios dwindle to almost worthless levels. We saw the firing and/or resignation of top executives even as they walked away with huge personal fortunes. And we saw the total U.S. stock market decline significantly, due partly to loss of confidence in U.S. corporations by both individual and institutional investors. In sum, a crisis of huge proportion.

> Think out the potential consequences of actions.

> "The obscure we see eventually, the completely apparent takes longer."
>
> —Edward R. Morrow

This story is still ongoing and likely to continue for some time. But enough of it played out in 2002 to make that year's events a sufficient case study for our purposes. So, the treatment here will be limited to a few major firms and to key events occurring just before or during that one year. Just enough detail will be provided to draw appropriate lessons about crisis management. The treatment of Enron will be the most detailed, partly because it is so rich in lessons, but also because it was the first case to surface. It started the domino effect that exposed bad practices at other firms.

The Enron Story

The bottom line on Enron is: The actions of a dishonest management group brought down a large company, its employees, and its investors. In so doing, they changed the firm's reputation from an example of exceptional innovation to the very definition of corruption.

Enron began in 1985, with the merger of Houston Natural Gas with InterNorth (a natural gas company in Nebraska). It remained essentially a natural gas provider for several years after the merger. Then it began trading, first natural gas commodities and later, electricity. This trading is what got it into trouble.

In the 1990s Enron literally revolutionized energy trading. It created a global energy trading network. In 1999 the company started an Internet trading system that, a year or so later, was handling over two billion dollars per day in trades. Its stock eventually hit a high of $90 per share.

It seemed too good to be true—and it was. And market analysts began to notice problems in its balance sheet. The reality—soon to be discovered—was that the company was using complicated off-balance-sheet partnerships to hide debt and inflate profits and, at the same time, enrich its key executives. Its fall came fast, and hard.

One series of events clearly illustrates the level of deception and culpability of Enron's leadership:

-   In mid-August 2001, Sherron Watkins (later named by *Time Magazine* as a Person of the Year 2002 for whistle blowing), an accountant in the finance division, sent a memo to CEO Kenneth Lay warning of potential accounting scandals at Enron.

-   At the same time, Lay sent an e-mail to Enron employees saying: "I have never felt better about the prospects for the company....our stock price has suffered over the last few months...(but) our performance has never been stronger, our business model has never been more robust; our growth has never been more certain."

-   In late August 2001, with the stock down to $37 per share, Lay again wrote to employees: "one of my highest priorities is to restore investor confidence in Enron. This should result in a significantly higher stock price."

-   By the time of this last message, Lay had sold $40 million of his personal Enron stock.

What deception! A CEO, recognizing his firm was in deep trouble, misled employees about the value of their investment and the security of their jobs—while enriching himself.

Events moved swiftly, and out of control. In mid-October, the SEC began investigating Enron's off-balance-sheet partnerships, and CFO Andrew Fastow, designer of those partnerships, took a leave of absence. And employees took a big hit: On 17 October their 401 (k) retirement plans were changed, preventing them from selling Enron stock for thirty days. Two weeks later, the stock had fallen to $11 per share. By the end of November, it had fallen to less than one dollar per share. And on December 2, 2001, Enron filed for Chapter 11 bankruptcy protection and laid off 4000 employees.

In January 2002, the Justice Department began its criminal investigation of Enron. Lay resigned on January 23. In February, Congress held hearings at which Lay and Fastow pleaded the Fifth Amendment. Jeffrey Skilling, who had been Enron's President and Chief Operating Officer from December 1996 to February 2001, and CEO for a brief time (February–August 2002), testified that he was unaware of the details of any partnerships created to inflate earnings and hide debt.

Investigations and new revelations continued throughout 2002, and the outcome for some key leaders is still pending at this writing. But regardless of the outcome of the criminal investigations and prosecutions, the damage is uncorrectable: A once great firm is ruined, most of its employees have lost their jobs and their savings, and importantly, the Enron crisis started a cycle of revelations that brought down other companies and senior managers and shook investor confidence in corporate America.

WorldCom

All of corporate America fell under increased scrutiny due to Enron's misdeeds. Companies were forced to greater transparency in their financial dealings and reporting. In this environment, WorldCom, the nation's second largest telecommunications company, was discovered to have artificially boosted profits. In June 2002, it announced that hiding $3.85 billion in expenses over five quarters enabled the company to show a net income of $1.38 billion in 2001, instead of a loss. This announcement was subsequently followed by their admitting that the misstated expenses were much higher: $9 billion. The firm filed for bankruptcy (the largest in U.S. history) in July 2002.

Arthur Anderson

The story of Arthur Anderson, a truly legendary accounting firm, is a sad one. As auditor for Enron, WorldCom, and others, it put its stamp of approval on faulty bookkeeping. Then, in January 2002, the firm admitted it had destroyed a number of documents relating to Enron, its largest client. For that deed, Anderson was indicted in March and convicted in June of obstruction of justice.

This verdict was later overturned, but that was small comfort to the 28,000 employees who lost their jobs—or even to the firm, which still had to fight shareholder lawsuits relating to its auditing work at Enron and elsewhere. The net result was that all the bad publicity caused a steady stream of client defections that spelled the downfall of Arthur Anderson. It should have come as no surprise. Anderson had been involved in a number of high-profile accounting scandals for a decade. It had paid nearly a quarter of a billion dollars to settle shareholder suits related to its accounting practices at Waste Management, Sunbeam, and Boston Market. Arthur Anderson was truly an accident ready to happen.

So, what happened to cause such a respected firm to drift so far off course? The consulting business happened. Twenty-five years ago, Anderson's primary work was in tax and auditing, which put it in the position of having to judge and sometimes countermand clients. But in the 1980s Anderson got into a much more lucrative business: management consulting, with many of the same clients it was auditing. At the same time, the culture of the firm changed drastically as it began to judge and reward auditors, not by the quality of their audits, but by their ability to generate consulting work. The result: Auditors approved aggressive accounting moves that ultimately led to the downfall of clients like Enron and WorldCom, which crossed the fuzzy boundary from aggressive to fraudulent practices.

How could that have been allowed to happen? Well, it was certainly a failure of leadership within the organization, plus lax oversight on the part of the Board, and a lot of greed all through the system.

Merrill Lynch

In May 2002, Merrill Lynch, the country's largest securities firm, paid $100 million to settle a conflict of interest case brought by the New York Attorney General. The suit alleged that the firm, in order to inflate fees, had encouraged investors to buy stocks that they were privately calling "dogs" and "disasters." The CEO resigned, and the firm agreed to change its analyst compensation system. This is another case of management failure—to articulate sound values, build a corporate culture to foster those values, and exercise appropriate management oversight. The firm, and the whole securities industry, lost credibility in the eyes of the investing public.

And so it went. The spotlight on American business continued to focus attention on unethical and illegal practices through the year. The treatment here provides some of the major highlights to give the flavor of the crisis. The stories of company misdeeds and accused executives filled the pages of the end-year issues of all the national newspapers and magazines. The January 13,

2003, issue of *Business Week* devoted ten tightly packed pages to the topics of "worst managers" and "perp walks." Though only a few of the stories are discussed here, this treatment of the crisis should be sufficient to help validate the principles discussed later.

> ### Your Turn
>
> In 2000, would you have thought a scandal like this could ever occur in U.S. corporations? Did it surprise you? Why?

U2 Spy Plane Crisis

In late April 1960, in the waning days of the second Eisenhower administration, hopes were high for an agreement with the Soviet Union that would slow the arms race. A joint US/USSR summit was schedule for mid-May, in Paris, with both parties expected to make important concessions.

But it was not to be! Hopes were derailed by an incident-turned-crisis through inept handling by the United States.

The broad outline of the event, known as the U2 Crisis, can be simply stated: The Russians shot down an American U2 plane on a reconnaissance mission over Soviet territory and captured the pilot (but did not immediately acknowledge they had him). Khrushchev (the Soviet leader), then baited Eisenhower into a series of false statements about the affair and, two weeks later, walked out of the summit conference when Eisenhower failed to apologize and promise to halt future flights.

The details of the event, summarized here, show clear mismanagement of the crisis by President Eisenhower:

- The plane was shot down on May 1, about two weeks before the scheduled summit.

- Eisenhower had been assured by the CIA that the plane, if hit, would self-destruct in the air. So he assumed the pilot, craft, and its film were all destroyed, and decided to take no action. He did not think Khrushchev would make an issue of this in view of the impending summit.

- But Eisenhower miscalculated. Khrushchev made a speech several days later saying the Russians had shot down the plane and blaming the U.S. military (but not Eisenhower personally). He did not mention at that point that the pilot had been captured.

- Again Eisenhower chose not to come clean. He did not think Khrushchev had any real evidence, and concluded that the nature of the mission and his own involvement could be kept secret. He authorized a statement by NASA saying one of their weather planes had reported problems and may have strayed into Soviet airspace—an inept cover-up attempt, because the Russians and others had been aware of reconnaissance flights for some time. U2 flights were a badly kept secret.

- The next day, Khrushchev showed photographs of a wrecked plane (which was actually not our U2) but still didn't say he had the pilot. Eisenhower continued to think the problem would go away.

- But on May 7, Khrushchev went public with the fact that the Russians had the pilot—alive!

- Eisenhower knew he was in trouble, but still thought he could avoid telling the whole truth. He authorized a press release by the State Department saying that the pilot had not been authorized to overfly the Soviet Union—a statement sure to be viewed with amusement.

- There followed a series of press reports in the United States citing clumsy handling of all this. Khrushchev kept up his angry rhetoric in an effort to extract some sort of "mea culpa" from the embarrassed Eisenhower. But he never got it.

- At the summit, when Khrushcv angrily demanded an apology and a promise to halt such flights, he did not get that either—and, with his delegation, he walked out.

In sum, the U2 incident turned into a crisis that was costly in both security and treasure—an avoidable crisis caused by misinformation and miscalculation on the part of the United States. And it wasn't the spying that caused the crisis (all nations know that all nations spy). It was the series of clumsy lies. We should have known better!

Your Turn

Do you think it is ever acceptable for the government to lie about its involvement in an international incident?

Cuban Missile Crisis
A Serious Situation Quickly Well-Handled

The Cuban missile crisis was serious because it brought the world very close to a full-scale nuclear war, arguably closer than at any time before or since. It was quickly handled (in thirteen days) because it had to be, and well handled since war was averted. A brief overview of the crisis is provided here, followed by a day-by-day account of major events and actions. The principle source for this overview is Robert Kennedy's book *Thirteen Days*, generally considered the most authentic treatment of this crisis.

In October 1962, U.S. reconnaissance flights over Cuba confirmed that the Soviet Union was in the process of installing medium-range and intermediate-range nuclear missiles on the island—close enough to hit major portions of the United States with little warning time and high accu-

> In a crisis, it is hard to know all the facts. Trust your gut.

> "Experts should be on tap but never on top."
>
> —Winston Churchill

racy. President John F. Kennedy was informed that the missiles could be operational in about ten days. He knew he could not permit such a powerful Soviet presence just off our coast, such a drastic shift in the nuclear balance of power. Throughout the thirteen days of the crisis, he never deviated from his initial judgment: The Soviet missiles had to be removed. Rejecting the advice of his military advisors for an air strike and invasion of Cuba, he declared a quarantine or naval blockade of Cuba and demanded the missiles be withdrawn. They were—and the nature, pace, and timing of Kennedy's actions over those two weeks have made this a classic case of good crisis management that continues to be studied for its lessons to this day.

First, a bit of background to put the crisis in context. Kennedy had succeeded Dwight Eisenhower, who was well liked and respected at home and abroad. The country felt safe and secure under Eisenhower—and for good reason. We were much stronger militarily than the Soviet Union and, at the time, enjoyed low inflation and low debt. However, there was a certain yearning in the country for a more activist role in world affairs. Kennedy came in as a young and vigorous leader with an appealing agenda: We will "bear any burden, oppose any foe....." Kennedy was a war hero (important fifteen years after World War II), smart, self-confident, and charismatic. He truly inspired the country, and he brought aboard an excellent team of advisors. He also came into office with a personal history of hostility toward Cuba's leader, Fidel Castro. And, importantly, he blundered badly early in his administration by supporting an unsuccessful invasion of Cuba by about 1500 Cuban exiles—known as the Bay of Pigs invasion.

The Bay of Pigs invasion, a CIA plan aimed at removing Castro, was approved originally by President Eisenhower. When Kennedy succeeded Eisenhower, he allowed the invasion preparations and execution to continue. The exiles landed at the Bay of Pigs in Cuba on April 17, 1961 and were soundly defeated by Castro's forces. Lots of mistakes caused this tragedy: Surprise was lost due to leaks, Kennedy refused to authorize U.S. air support, and the general uprising against Castro (predicted by the CIA) did not materialize. Kennedy publicly assumed full responsibility for the invasion and its failure. A bad start for his presidency, but he learned an important lesson: Don't trust the experts. The Soviets derived two lessons: that Kennedy wasn't a very capable leader (which turned out to be a misjudgment), and that Castro might eventually be overthrown by the United States if they did not act in some way to prevent it. The action they took to protect Cuba and to improve their nuclear balance of power versus the United States was to put nuclear missiles in Cuba. So—though Kennedy did a good job of dealing with the crisis, he also had a hand in creating it.

Some key events during the crisis follow:

- *October 16 (Day #1)*

  Early in the morning, the President was informed that a U2 spy plane had acquired solid photographic evidence that the Soviet Union was installing medium-range and intermediate-range offensive missiles in Cuba, capable of hitting the United States. This was being done despite assurances by the Soviets that they would not deploy offensive weapons there, and Kennedy's public statements that we'd act to remove the weapons if they did.

  Kennedy quickly assembled a carefully selected team of advisors, called the ExComm (Executive Committee of the National Security Council). The group agreed that they had to find a way to get the missiles removed. They also decided to try to keep their knowledge and planning secret for as long as possible so as not to tip their hand to the Soviets.

- *October 17 (Day #2)–October 21 (Day #6)*

  Much discussion and in-fighting occurred in the ExComm. They debated the three military options: air strike, invasion, and blockade. The blockade option steadily developed increasing support for several reasons: The Air Force could not guarantee that an air strike would destroy all the missiles, an air strike followed by invasion might provoke the Soviets to act against U.S. interests elsewhere (e.g., Berlin), and the air strike/invasion options could start a nuclear exchange. The potentially adverse international reaction to the United States attacking a small country was also a factor favoring a blockade. However, the merits of the various options continued to be debated for several days. A definite decision to blockade was reached on Saturday, October 21.

- *October 22 (Day #7)*

  This was the day the President made his televised speech (at 7:00 p.m.) informing the nation and the world of the situation and the intended U.S. response. Prior to the speech, he briefed congressional leaders and had some key allies informed. His speech pulled no punches. He stated what the Soviets had done and was specific about the danger the missiles posed to the United States and the whole western hemisphere. He announced the blockade of Cuba, said further action would be taken if the missiles were not removed, and specified that any nuclear missiles fired from Cuba against any nation in the western hemisphere would be regarded as an attack by the Soviets on the United States calling for a full retaliatory strike against the Soviet Union.

- *October 23 (Day #8)*

  This day saw tough talk from the Soviets. President Kennedy sent his brother, Robert Kennedy (the Attorney General) to speak to Russian Ambassador Dobrynin to impress on him the seriousness of the U.S. intentions: We would definitely stop Soviet ships at the blockade line. Later that night, at the suggestion of British Ambassador David Ormsby-Gore, the President contracted the arc of the blockade from 800 to 500 miles to give the Soviets a bit more time to reflect.

- *October 24 (Day #9)*

  This was a very tense day. The blockade went into effect at 10:00 a.m. The ExComm was in session and first received a report that two Russian ships and a submarine were approaching the blockade line, and then a second report that they had suddenly stopped. Shortly thereafter, some twenty Russian ships close to the barrier stopped or turned back. The President ordered the Navy not to board any ships. He wanted to give the Russians plenty of time and opportunity to back off. One Russian tanker (the *Bucharest*) was allowed to proceed toward Cuba because it was judged unlikely to be carrying any kind of missiles or contraband.

- *October 25 (Day #10)*

  In a dramatic televised confrontation with Russian Ambassador Zorin at the United Nations, U.S. Ambassador Adlai Stevenson revealed the U.S. evidence (the photographs). This was a necessary step because much of the world was not convinced that the Soviets had placed missiles in Cuba. This convinced everyone.

  This same night, to convince the Soviets that he intended to enforce the blockade, the President carefully selected a ship for boarding: the *Marucla*—an American-built, Panamanian-owned, Lebanese-registered, Soviet-chartered ship, captained by a Greek. It wasn't likely to be carrying military equipment, but the next morning a U.S. armed boarding party went aboard and inspected. Our point was made: We would stop ships.

- *October 26 (Day #11)*

  A breakthrough in communications occurred. John Scali, an ABC reporter, was called by the Soviet KGB station chief, Aleksandra Fomin. They met, and Fomin asked Scali to approach the administration with a proposed solution: The Soviets would remove the missiles under United Nations supervision if the United States would lift the blockade and pledge not to invade Cuba. A similar proposal was made in a letter that day from Khrushchev to Kennedy.

- *October 27 (Day #12)*

  A second letter from Khrushchev was received, adding the requirement that the United States remove its missiles based in Turkey. Members of the ExComm were confused and worried. Why this second letter? And how should the two letters be handled? The reality was that the United States was already intending to remove those missiles, but the President decided that he would not remove them under duress as a part of any agreement over Cuba.

  In the midst of deliberations over how to handle the two letters, another event took place: Our U2 plane flying over Cuba was shot down by a surface-to-air missile. The U.S. military wanted to retaliate, but the President kept his cool, saying he was not going to war because some junior officer in Cuba pushed a button by mistake.

In a skillful political move, the President decided to answer the first letter received from Khrushchev, accepting the terms proposed, and ignoring the letter mentioning Turkey. The letter was sent, and simultaneously Robert Kennedy met again with Ambassador Dobrynin and informed him of the U.S. decision. He told Dobrynin that the missiles in Turkey would be removed later, but could not be a part of this agreement.

- *October 28 (Day #13)*

  At 9:00 a.m. Washington time, Khrushchev, in a radio broadcast, accepted the American terms: He would remove the missiles; we would agree not to invade Cuba. A crisis put to rest—a war averted.

The Cuban Missile Crisis has always been considered one of the best historical examples of skillful crisis management. Many factors played a part in the successful outcome: Patient leaders (on both sides), good advisors, the skillful use of multiple communication links—but most of all a U.S. President, well versed in military matters and international diplomacy, who saw the problem clearly and took timely and appropriate action. Many other specific lessons from this case are mentioned later in this module under the appropriate principles.

Your Turn

How do you think President George W. Bush and his team would have handled the Cuban Missile Crisis?

Memogate: The Crisis at CBS (September 2004)

This crisis occurred in September 2004, in the midst of the hotly contested presidential race between President George W. Bush and Senator John Kerry.

For many years, Bush's service in the Air National Guard during the Vietnam War had been the subject of controversy. Rumors would surface from time to time that he had received preferential treatment.

> "Bad news does not improve with age."
>
> —Robert Gerard

However, in September 2004, this story was out of the headlines—replaced by controversies over John Kerry's Vietnam service.

Enter CBS and news anchor Dan Rather—with a potential bombshell story against Bush on the September 8 broadcast of *60 Minutes Wednesday*. The story presented four memos, allegedly written by Bush's commander during his service—as evidence that he received preferential treatment in the Texas Air National Guard.

The authenticity of the memos was immediately challenged on the Internet, on television, and in the press because the typeface used was rare in typewriters at that time. CBS immediately went into crisis mode, and on a very slippery slope. They continued to defend the story for twelve days, despite emerging evidence that the documents were bogus.

A few facts and milestones shed some light on the affair:

- Mary Maples (producer of the segment) and Rather had been looking into Bush's service since 1999. Then, suddenly, Maples was informed that a retired Lieutenant Colonel from the Texas Air National Guard (Bill Burkett) might have some new documentation.

- Maples met with Burkett on September 2 and received some of the memos, then the remainder a few days later. A story was born!

- The *60 Minutes* segment was originally intended to air on September 29. But sensing blood in the water, and fearing she'd be scooped by other news sources, Maples pushed to have it aired on September 8. CBS executives and Dan Rather agreed, trusting that the usually reliable Maples had fully checked the story.

- But Maples had made a number of serious mistakes: She ignored the fact that Burkett was a longstanding critic of Bush. She failed to determine the source of the documents. She ignored the statements by four document examiners and others consulted that the memos could not be authenticated. Finally, she did not obey the instructions of concerned CBS news president Andrew Heyward—to be sure to get the story right.

CBS compounded the problem of a false story by continuing to publicly defend it long after all other news sources and the general public had become absolutely convinced that the documents were fraudulent. The defense continued until September 20 when CBS finally disavowed the story and appointed an independent panel to investigate.

The panel's report in early January 2005 was highly critical of CBS and recommended the firing of Maples and three other executives. Dan Rather announced his voluntary retirement as CBS news anchor shortly before the report was released.

CBS was criticized in the report for "myopic zeal" to be first with the story, "failing miserably" to authenticate the documents, being overzealous in defending the story after serious questions surfaced, and making false and misleading statements in that defense.

In summary, this was a case of top executives too trusting or asleep while a producer bypassed established vetting procedures and threw caution to the winds. They thus missed the opportunity to prevent the crisis. Their mismanagement of the aftermath created a credibility crisis for the whole CBS organization that many feel will be hard to outlive.

Your Turn

Why do you think CBS was so slow to acknowledge its mistake?

The Catholic Church Crisis:
A Case of Sexual Abuse of Children and Young People by Clergy

This crisis is well known and well documented. It was on the front pages of newspapers and on nightly TV during much of 2002, and continues to be news years later. It has often been called the greatest crisis in the history of the Catholic Church. As a committed Catholic, I describe it here reluctantly and with a heavy heart. But it is included because it is a case particularly rich in lessons about crisis management.

The essence of the story is as follows: Over five decades, more than 4000 priests were accused of sexually molesting children and young people—and the church hierarchy (the bishops) did not take sufficient action to address the issue. In many cases, accused priests were transferred from parish to parish, where they continued to prey on the young.

> The truth will ultimately be known. In a crisis tell it all, tell it promptly.

> "Smart leaders believe only half of what they hear. Discerning leaders know which half to believe."
>
> —John C. Maxwell

While cases of pedophilia (child sexual abuse) received a lot of publicity, most of the cases involved the sexual abuse of teenage boys and young men by homosexual priests. This problem is not unique to the Catholic Church, and it may be less prevalent in the Church than in society as a whole. But it reached crisis proportions for three reasons: First, it proved to be much more widespread than anyone had ever suspected; second, since the offenders were in positions of trust, this represented a morally irresponsible abuse of authority; and finally, the problem was so ineptly handled by the bishops. This combination of factors produced nearly unanimous outrage among American Catholics.

A more detailed chronology of events is necessary to appreciate the full nature and scope of this crisis. The problem has existed in the Church to some degree for decades. But the first big case that received national attention occurred in 1985. A priest in Louisiana was tried and convicted of multiple counts of sexual molestation. This case got the attention of some bishops and led to reform efforts in some dioceses. Another case of serial molestation by a priest in Rhode Island, in 1991, underlined the gravity of the situation. As a result, the National Conference of Catholic Bishops, in 1992, proposed a policy to deal with this problem that included: swift action on accusations, suspension of priests when accusations were credible, full cooperation with the police, and support for victims. However, the policy had no teeth because the

Conference could not compel compliance, and many bishops just ignored the policy.

The event that brought this crisis to national attention was the case of John Geoghan, a defrocked Boston priest and serial child abuser. Though hundreds of accusations were leveled against Geoghan, most were barred from criminal prosecution by the statute of limitations. But, in January 2002, he was convicted of indecent assault of a 10-year-old boy—and, importantly, the *Boston Globe* got a court-ordered release of the Church's files on this case. These files revealed that this one priest had been credibly accused of abusing over a hundred young boys over a period of three decades, and that he had been transferred by the bishop to three different parishes during that time.

As the crisis quickly escalated, victims came forward from all over the country. When the media picked up the scent of real malfeasance and dug deeper into the facts, it quickly became obvious that this was not just a Boston problem, but a Church-wide problem. A few of the specific revelations during 2002 indicate the scope of the problem:

- The Diocese of Tucson settled eleven civil lawsuits alleging abuse of sixteen plaintiffs by four priests.

- The Diocese of Manchester, New Hampshire, gave local prosecutors the names of fourteen priests accused of sexual abuse.

- The Bishop of Palm Beach, Florida, resigned after admitting he'd sexually abused a fifteen-year-old seminarian in 1975.

- The Diocese of Cleveland announced that nine priests were under investigation for sexual abuse of minors and that another twelve had been removed from active ministry because of similar charges.

And so it went. All during 2002: revelation upon revelation, all over the country.

The list of offenders continued to grow. Hundreds of instances involving hundreds of priests, and estimates of hundreds of millions in ultimate settlement costs. And always the same theme: Bishops allowing offenders to remain in active ministry. Importantly too, the scandal gradually shifted focus: from simply targeting abusive priests to revealing cover-ups by bishops who protected them and paid huge sums to hide the problem. And it all happened so quickly. A few months into 2002, the situation had crystallized into a rightfully embarrassed Church hierarchy and a very angry laity demanding a solution.

The problem demanded action—and got it! In April, the thirteen U.S. cardinals were called to a special summit meeting at the Vatican and heard Pope

John Paul II declare: "There is no room in the priesthood and religious life for those who would harm the young."

The cardinals returned from Rome realizing that prompt action was essential and quickly announced that this crisis would be *the* subject of the scheduled meeting of the Conference of Catholic Bishops in June 2002, in Dallas, Texas. Prior to the Rome meeting, it was just going to be *one* of many topics discussed in Dallas.

The bishops suffered no delusions by the time of the June meeting. Their President, Bishop Wilton D. Gregory, summed it up for them with this statement: "The crisis, in truth, is about a profound loss of confidence by the faithful in our leadership as shepherds, because of our failures in addressing the crime of the sexual abuse of children and young people by priests."

Tough action was indeed taken at that meeting. The U.S. bishops adopted a "Charter for the Protection of Children and Young People"—essentially a "zero tolerance" policy. Plus, they established a National Review Board, headed by a layman (Oklahoma Governor Frank Keating) to monitor compliance. They also established a National Office for Child and Youth Protection under Kathleen McChesney, the third ranking official in the Federal Bureau of Investigation. The policy was then forwarded to the Vatican where, with some minor modifications, it was approved in December 2002, making it binding on all U.S. bishops (some of whom had actually begun implementation right after the Dallas meeting).

However, there is more to this story. By the time of the Dallas meeting in June more than 200 priests had been removed from ministry. On November 11, 2002, *USA Today* published a list of 234 priests from the 10 largest U.S. dioceses that had been accused of sexual abuse of a minor. Most of the other 184 U.S. dioceses were known to be touched by this problem in some way. By year's end, over 300 priests had been forced to leave their ministry or the priesthood. So the problem was obviously truly nationwide.

Boston continued to be a major focal point due to the sheer numbers involved and the continuing stream of revelations of mishandling by Cardinal Bernard Law. By December 2002, nearly 140 lawsuits involving Geoghan victims had been settled by the Boston Archdiocese, and over 400 other lawsuits had been filed in behalf of alleged victims of other Boston priests. It was reported that the archdiocese was considering filing for Chapter 11 bankruptcy protection. The Massachusetts Attorney General sent Cardinal Law a grand jury subpoena. Outrage grew among Catholic laity, and finally, in an unprecedented move, fifty-eight Boston priests signed a petition calling for Law to step down. After meeting with the Pope, Cardinal Law did resign on December 13, 2002.

As part of its continuing effort to deal with the crisis, the Catholic Church commissioned an independent study by the John Jay College of Criminal Justice. The conclusions of this study, reported on February 27, 2004, were that during the period from 1950 to 2002, 10,667 minor victims accused 4,392 priests of sexual abuse. Eighty-one percent of the victims were male, and only two percent of the accused priests received prison sentences.

What will happen in the future? It's hard to say. There continue to be additional revelations and settlements around the country, and human nature being what it is, we can expect some occasional new incidents over time. But the Catholic Church in the future is likely to be a very inhospitable place for a priest inclined to sexual abuse of minors, for many reasons: The charter, now approved by the Vatican, binds all bishops to enforce a no-tolerance policy. There is strong lay oversight to ensure compliance. And, most important, the bishops having acknowledged their past mistakes are not likely to repeat them. The new rules are likely to give potential offenders pause; plus, reforms in the selection and training of seminarians are already in progress. All this will help. But there remains a serious problem: Lack of confidence in the hierarchy and leadership of the Catholic Church. Though the church has now taken strong steps to limit future incidents, its poor judgment in the past will be difficult to live down. A good deal of its moral authority has been lost, which makes this a continuing crisis for the Catholic Church.

This was a crisis poorly handled—thus deserving of study. The Church made many mistakes in handling the crisis: The bishops underestimated its severity and complexity, failed to appreciate the need to act quickly, consulted inadequate sources for advice, and lost their moral compass. In their attempt to rehabilitate priests and protect the short-term reputation of the Church, they ignored their responsibility to protect the young and thus tarnished the long-term credibility of the Church. They also failed to appreciate an important truth about most crises: They don't improve with age—they require action to resolve.

Your Turn

How long do you think it will take the Catholic Church to recover from this crisis? What would you recommend the Church do to speed that recovery?

Summary

- The crisis state is too often the normal state for today's organizations.
- A crisis can destroy an organization.
- Good leadership in crisis can save an organization.
- Managing crises:
    - Is necessary and possible
    - Requires early recognition
    - Demands deep leader involvement
    - Calls for deliberate intervention strategies

Chapter 7

Principles for Managing Crises

Objectives

- Recognize the need for a deliberate strategy or tool to prevent and/or manage crises.
- Understand twenty-six principles useful in preventing and/or managing crises.
- Learn to use the principles as a tool to prevent and/or manage crises.

This chapter provides a set of principles for crisis management. Twenty-six principles are identified: six to prevent and prepare for crises and twenty to guide action during crises. The lengthy list of actions during crises is organized under three headings: Getting Organized and Oriented, Developing a Course of Action, and Implementing the Plan. The principles are listed on the next page.

Each principle is stated in the form of an action step, then discussed briefly and validated by one or more of the six cases in Chapter 6. The set of principles represents a framework or lens to view crises—and a tool for the leader to effectively manage crises.

PRINCIPLES FOR CRISIS MANAGEMENT

Actions to Prevent and Prepare for Crises

1. Lean forward/anticipate crises.
2. Assemble the right team.
3. Strengthen intelligence capabilities.
4. Exercise the crisis management system.
5. Set the climate: Balance urgency with calm.
6. Act early.

Actions during Crises

Getting Organized and Oriented

7. Be mindful of history.
8. Tailor the team.
9. Orient the team thoroughly.
10. Seek reliable facts.
11. Never assume you have the full facts.
12. Assess status of allies and adversaries.

Developing a Course of Action

13. Be true to your values.
14. Play worst-case scenarios.
15. Take a long-term view.
16. Don't act on impulse—stay calm.
17. State objectives clearly.

Implementing the Plan

18. React in a timely way.
19. Carefully prepare your first public statement.
20. Continuously expand communications linkages.
21. Recognize no long-term secrecy is possible.
22. Promptly acknowledge mistakes and correct mis-statements.
23. Stay focused.
24. Balance tenacity with flexibility.
25. Stay calm.
26. Learn as you go—and after the crisis.

Actions to Prevent and Prepare for Crises

1. *Lean forward/anticipate crises.*

To be asleep is to be vulnerable. To be awake and alert is to be prepared. In the life of all organizations, crises will threaten from time to time. Wary, alert organizations are more likely to sense a dangerous environment early and deal with it before it develops into a crisis. They are always asking the questions: What can go wrong, and what can we do now to prevent it?

> "While failing to prepare you are preparing to fail."
> —Benjamin Franklin

- For decades the *Catholic Church* had encountered incidents of sexual abuse by clergy. Efforts to deal with the problem proved inadequate over time. Cases proliferated, rehabilitation efforts failed, and settlement costs mounted. It's fair to ask why the Church did not ask itself, along the way: What are we doing wrong? If we don't get a grip on it, won't it eventually get totally out of control and be a huge crisis? The failure to anticipate this crisis has cost the Church heavily, in treasure and credibility.

- CBS executives did not act to prevent *Memogate* even though a number of early warning signs of trouble surfaced.

- After Tylenol contamination was discovered, *Johnson & Johnson* designed packaging to prevent reoccurrence. But should not all industries be anticipating safety problems (e.g., the possibility of contamination of food products or drugs; automotive safety problems; safety of children's toys)? And shouldn't they act to put safety ahead of profits, before a problem occurs? Johnson & Johnson's long-term reputation for social responsibility and prompt ethical action helped it surmount this crisis with minimum damage. But it is far better to anticipate problems and act preemptively to prevent them.

2. *Assemble the right team.*

You can't manage anything well without good people. And crises are special situations requiring the very best people. It is the senior leader's job to attract a quality team, capable of handling not just routine work but the most severe crises.

- The *Corporate Malfeasance Crisis* occurred in large part because of the failure of the top teams (Boards of Directors) to fulfill their responsibilities for selection of ethical senior leaders and for oversight of plans and operations.

- The *Catholic Church* would probably have gotten the advice necessary to prevent its crisis if its top team had been constructed properly. The Church relied heavily on the advice of clerics (who worried about the welfare of fellow priests), doctors (whose emphasis was on rehabilitation of abusive priests), and lawyers (whose concern was helping the Church avoid scandal and lawsuits). What was lacking on the teams was a strong lay component that would push to put the welfare of children above all else.

- Eisenhower's team should have warned him of the risks of being caught in a lie over the *U2 Incident*. Kennedy's team should not have been so positive about the assumptions that predicted success of the *Bay of Pigs* invasion. Both of these crises had multiple causes—but faulty team advice played a big part.

3. *Strengthen intelligence capabilities.*

Continuous scanning of the external environment of the organization is necessary to anticipate potential problems. Effective scanning requires the means to look and the capability to draw meaning from what is found. Building intelligence capabilities means getting the necessary people and technology to find the dots and connect them. It is not sufficient to simply assemble valuable fragmentary information. It must be integrated into a whole—to see patterns sufficiently well to predict vulnerabilities.

- The *9/11 terrorist attacks* provide a lesson here. In spite of many warnings over more than a decade, the United States allowed its intelligence capabilities to deteriorate, both technological and human intelligence resources. Findings from Congressional investigations tell the story: FBI missions and equipment not adequate for the threat, NSA lacking in translators, and a lack of information exchange among agencies. We could not see all the dots, and we lacked the organization to connect those we could see.

- In the *Corporate Malfeasance* case, thorough board oversight would have recognized the danger of an accounting firm like Arthur Anderson rendering both auditing and consulting services. After the fact that seems so obvious—so why not before the fact, as scanning took place for potential problems? Probably because no one was really looking or asking the right questions.

-   In approving the *Bay of Pigs invasion*, Kennedy relied on the intelligence estimate that the invasion would cause a popular revolt in Cuba. This did not occur. Someone saw dots that were not there.

Building effective intelligence systems is difficult due to parochialism and turf-guarding among participating organizations and groups, and because building a strong system is expensive. Multiple priorities are always competing for resources. The path of least resistance is often taken: fund the most immediate pressing needs at the expense of resources to predict future problems. That's where real leadership is needed—to bite the bullet and sell it to others—to take the long view to hedge against disaster.

4. *Exercise the crisis management system.*

Planning for crises must include periodic evaluation of the organization's crisis management capabilities. The team's scanning operations to detect potential threats need to be extended to play "what-if" games—well before any crisis occurs. Assuming worse-case scenarios and doing contingency planning serves three purposes: (1) Teamwork is improved through real-life exercises, (2) leaders can assess their team's capability, and (3) the exercises can produce useful contingency plans to guide the organization in crisis. Thus, exercising the system not only helps in crisis prevention, it also helps train the team to function in crisis.

-   The *Corporate Malfeasance* case abounds in ignored opportunities to avoid disaster by asking "what-if" questions, the most critical being: What happens to us as individuals, to the company, and to our employees if the public finds out we falsified earnings, created dummy corporations, burned records, and sold stock early at a profit? Playing out the various scenarios—all the way to jail—would have been a useful exercise for senior leaders and their teams.

-   Similarly, some serious "what-if" questions within the *Catholic Church* would probably have alerted the bishops to their precarious course: What happens if the people find out we've transferred bad priests and paid out huge sums in hush money? What happens if the legal authorities discover we have failed to report crimes? What might happen to us—and the Church we serve?

5.   *Set the climate: Balance urgency with calm.*

This is one of the toughest tasks of the leader at every stage of a crisis, including the moment of first discovery. Crises demand urgency. They rarely get better without action, and sooner is usually better than later. So, leaders need to keep urgency on the front burner for the whole team. It is difficult to achieve during the time of only faint warning and becomes increasingly difficult when a crisis drags on for long periods—but it must be done.

The atmosphere of urgency can cause stress. People and systems perform differently under stress, and usually not as effectively. So, fostering an atmosphere of calm amid all the turmoil is another leadership task. It doesn't happen by accident. The leader must not only *be* calm; but he or she must *seem* calm and find ways to encourage calm in others.

In sum, balancing urgency and calm is an important leadership task, and tricky. Too much calm can be read as a lack of urgency; lack of calm hurts team performance. Balance is the key.

-   In the *Corporate Malfeasance* case, the Bush Administration and Congress acted very quickly against individual offenders and were exceptionally fast in passing legislation to reform corporate reporting and accounting practices. This kept the crisis from becoming more severe. It was important that public confidence in the honesty of the financial system be restored. At this writing, there are still many forces pressing hard on a struggling stock market, and there are still occasional incidents of corporate malfeasance. But in this instance, government urgency has paid off. CEO's may not be any more honest, but most are probably quite wary of cheating or fudging numbers.

-   In a short duration and very dangerous crisis, a sense of urgency is easy to achieve, but calm may be hard to maintain. All accounts of the *Cuban Missile Crisis* depict President Kennedy as a model executive: urgent but calm in crisis. This had an impact on his team, the nation, and undoubtedly the favorable outcome.

-   On the other hand, President Eisenhower during the developing *U2 Crisis* maintained extraordinary calm but did not sense the urgency of the situation, which caused a bad outcome.

-   In the *Catholic Church* case, there was initially a lack of urgency on the part of the bishops. Even in the winter of 2001–2002, as the crisis deepened, they merely said it would be "an" agenda item at their June 2002 meeting in Dallas. However, before the meeting, the American cardinals were summoned to Rome. When they returned from meeting with the

Pope, a new sense of urgency was apparent, and the June meeting was solely devoted to the subject of sexual abuse by clergy. Many disagree with the actions taken in Dallas, but one thing is certain: There was much more urgency than would have occurred without the summons to Rome—and this urgency improved the crisis environment.

6. *Act early.*

Timing is important, as is balance. Premature action without the facts and appropriate deliberation must be avoided. But the greatest mistakes seem to occur from inaction or late action.

- Had the *Catholic Church* acted promptly, decades ago, to examine their practices for priest selection and training and the results of their early failed efforts at rehabilitation, it could have avoided its crisis.

- In *Memogate*, the damage to the reputation of CBS would have been lessened significantly had they acted early to acknowledge their mistake rather than defend the story for twelve days.

- Had Eisenhower immediately acknowledged that we had *U2* reconnaissance flights over Russia (which the Soviets knew anyway), there would likely have been no crisis over this affair. But his evasive and cumbersome handling of things derailed an important diplomatic initiative.

Your Turn

In the organizations where you have worked, have there been deliberate and adequate measures taken to prevent and prepare for crisis?

Actions during Crises

Getting Organized and Oriented

7. *Be mindful of history.*

Few problems are totally new. Taking time to reflect on the lessons from past crises can provide valuable guidance. Yet this is not easily done. Some leaders lack the necessary curiosity. Also, reflection

> "Before everything else, getting ready is the secret of success."
> —Henry Ford

takes time—a scarce commodity, particularly in the early stages of a crisis. But the thoughtful leader must find the time, so essential to perspective.

-   President Kennedy was an avid reader of history. At the time of the *Cuban Missile Crisis* he was reading the book, *The Guns of August* by Barbara Tuckman—about how World War I was brought about by a series of avoidable miscalculations. The book guided his thinking all during the crisis. The late Hugh Sidy wrote this in a piece titled "History On His Shoulder" in *Time* magazine:

    "What shouts to us over these years is that Kennedy saw the missile crisis in a worldwide tapestry of what had been, what was, and what would be. The lessons of history were always at the forefront of his mind...when Kennedy first saw the pictures of the missiles in place, he felt that the U.S. would have to launch a full-scale assault on Cuba to destroy them. History, riding on his shoulder, held him back. First, learn more. Then communicate. Don't humiliate. Be patient. And strong."

-   History should have alerted *CBS* to be extra cautious in vetting their story. During the two years preceding the CBS broadcast, top editors at *The New York Times* and *USA Today* had been forced to resign over fabricated stories.

-   Had the leaders of the *Catholic Church* and the executives involved in the *Corporate Malfeasance* case taken time to look back at past crises, they might have found and focused on the lessons of Watergate: Bad situations rarely improve with age, the truth ultimately comes out, leaders can be brought down by poorly handled crises, and top people can go to jail. Such historical perspective might have awakened some to their responsibilities and their vulnerabilities.

8. *Tailor the team.*

The need for a good team was mentioned earlier as an action to prevent and prepare for crises. Once a crisis occurs, that team may need some redesign to fit the specific situation. The optimum team membership is influenced by such things as new information needs, group dynamics, and political considerations. The leader may need to both add and remove members as a crisis develops.

-   During the *Cuban Missile Crisis*, Kennedy personally picked the members of the ExComm. Some members of his cabinet were not included. Some outsiders were added for various reasons, such as their insights on the Soviet Union or their political or diplomatic value. His press secretary was purposely left out of any deliberations so as not to put him in a position of lying to the press. Some outsiders, like U.N. Representative Adlai Stevenson and former Secretary of State Dean Atcheson, were brought in for certain meetings. Congress was totally excluded until the day the President went public with the story.

- As the *Catholic Church Crisis* deepened, the bishops should have added lay persons to their teams to provide diversity of views.

- In the *Corporate Malfeasance* case, the lack of independent directors contributed to the poor oversight that permitted the crisis to start and grow out of control.

- During the course of the country's war on terror, the Bush Administration has often been cited as having warring factions (e.g., Powell versus Rumsfeld). But a key point was lost on the critics: Healthy conflict is exactly what you need in a crisis. It's the source of creativity. And the bigger and more complicated the crisis, the more you need that conflict.

9. *Orient the team thoroughly.*

Team members can't read the leader's mind. Orientation is necessary to draw the best from even the most capable team. A leader owes the team certain critical orientation elements: What he expects, any boundaries he wants to place on the team, any "musts" that should guide thinking, and the part the leader will play personally in the deliberations. Also, it is through the orientation process that leaders can encourage candor and, if appropriate, demand secrecy.

- The *Cuban Missile Crisis* is instructive on this point. From the start, Kennedy made clear his objective: Get the missiles out of Cuba without provoking a war. That objective guided ExComm deliberations. Kennedy also handled the ExComm skillfully. Heeding his brother's advice to avoid intimidating the group, he deliberately absented himself from certain meetings. But he tapped into the discussions at critical times with questions and guidance, either personally or through his brother.

- The *Arthur Anderson* employees who burned Enron documents thought they were protecting their firm. How wrong they were! There would have been a more favorable outcome for the firm if, early-on, its top leadership had passed the word: Play it straight and cooperate fully with the investigation. It worked for Johnson & Johnson in the *Tylenol Crisis*.

10. *Seek reliable facts.*

What the leader needs is an accurate diagnosis of the causes and status of the crisis situation and the feasibility and likely outcomes of various actions. Getting that requires leaders who know enough to ask the right questions and assess the reliability of their sources. They must seek to identify the uncertainties in any facts. They must acknowledge what they don't know and plan to fill the gaps. Getting reliable facts is tough, creative work. Getting the right team in place is the first step: a team with the correct blend of expertise, diversity, and candor to generate the necessary conflict—for conflict (differences in viewpoint) is what you need when the chips are down in a complex problem environment.

- In the *Cuban Missile Crisis* President Kennedy was always conscious of the bad advice he'd gotten from the military in the *Bay of Pigs* incident. This led him to be much more skeptical and to ask tough questions regarding facts presented: When will the missiles be operational? Whose estimate is that? How do you know those are nuclear warheads? Can an air strike take out all the missiles?

  As mentioned earlier, he was also conscious that his presence sometimes inhibited candor, so he placed his brother in the role of "informal agitator" and asked everyone to assume the role of "critical evaluator" of the various courses of action.

- In *Memogate*, the failure to get the facts straight was the single most important cause of the crisis. With the right facts, CBS would not have aired the story.

- In the *Catholic Church Crisis*, the bishops were given optimistic predictions by medical authorities about their ability to rehabilitate abusive priests. Events would have turned out differently had the bishops pressed the issue: How reliable is that prediction, and how do you know?

11. *Never assume you have the full facts.*

The truth is always a moving target. Thus, the search for facts in a crisis must be continuous. You will always be discovering something new that changes the diagnosis or the plan of action.

- One crisis not described here, but one sure to be recalled by all, is the *Sniper Crisis* in the Washington, D.C. area in the Fall of 2002. It is a good example of facts and assumptions changing daily: Was it one person or more? Where did he/she/they live? What kind of car was used? What was the motive for the shootings? Law enforcement officials kept pressing for new facts throughout the several weeks of this crisis. Only in the final few days did the facts all come together sufficiently to place the all-points bulletin that resulted in capture of the killers.

- In the *Cuban Missile Crisis*, Kennedy never knew that the Soviets had short-range tactical nuclear weapons in Cuba and that local commanders had authority to use them if the United States mounted an invasion force. It was not until many years after the crisis that this was revealed. Had Kennedy known this, he would have concluded that invasion of Cuba was not one of his options, since it would have surely triggered a nuclear exchange.

- Eisenhower was operating with all the wrong facts in the *U2 Crisis:* that the Russians did not know about the U2 flights, that the U2 would self-destruct, and that our pilot could not be in Russian hands. Eisenhower was asleep on this one. The lack of full facts led him to some very serious blunders—and he lacked the facts because he did not keep original facts and assumptions under review.

12. *Assess status of allies and adversaries.*

This is a special case of fact finding, and so important it is best handled as a separate principle. It includes assessment of the capabilities, limitations, and the degree of cooperation or opposition of all involved elements: individuals, organizations, agencies, and nations. No easy task.

Skepticism is always in order. Alliances and friendships do not hold for all situations. Forces shift sides at times. There often seems to be a bias against cooperation and coordination even among those with similar objectives. Values, desires, traditions, technical capability, pressures, and mandates—all play a part and must be assessed in light of any given crisis. Nothing can be taken for granted.

- In the *Catholic Church Crisis*, the bishops always felt that they had enough moral authority to keep the support of lay Catholics. However, once their role in mishandling sexual abuse cases was revealed, they lost that support. Lay activism in the matter deepened their crisis. Had they continually assessed that support during the decades of this developing crisis, they might have anticipated their control slipping and acted to avert the crisis.

-   The *Cuban Missile Crisis* illustrates the added complexity of assessing the status of friends and foes in international crises. Kennedy was quite conscious of his level of support and opposition within his administration and with the Congress, the American people, and traditional allies. He worked hard and successfully to build support within such bodies as the Organization of American States and the United Nations. However, in dealing with the Soviets, many uncertainties arose during the crisis: What was Khrushchev like? What was he thinking? What pressures were on him? And (at one point) was he still in charge? A review of that case indicates Kennedy kept addressing these questions, but uncertainties remained and complicated the crisis.

Your Turn

Think of some crisis you have observed in an organization. Were any of the six principles for getting organized ignored? Which ones? What was the impact?

Developing a Course of Action

13. *Be true to your values.*

Values, our "shoulds," are intended to guide us at all times. They are usually developed and articulated in quiet times, and find easy application in periods of low stress. But crises put us to a test. Can we stick to our values under stress? We'd better. Often our values are all we have to guide us through troubled waters. Good leaders know that and act on it.

> "Wisdom requires the long view."
>
> —John F. Kennedy

- One of the first things Johnson & Johnson executives did when the *Tylenol Crisis* occurred was examine their mission statement. It told them they were wedded to socially responsible action. They stuck to that credo, and it paid off by enhancing the firm's reputation.

- Certainly, the bishops of the *Catholic Church* always cared about the protection of children and the Church's long-term credibility. But faced with sexual abuse incidents, they allowed their values to shift to the rehabilitation of offending priests and the short-term reputation of the Church. This shift in values led to the actions that produced the crisis.

- In the early days of the *Cuban Missile Crisis*, many ExComm members who advocated an air strike or invasion of Cuba were turned around when one member said: "We have to remember who we are." Suddenly, values guided the discussion.

- In *Memogate*, CBS, in its urgency to be first with the story, ignored its most fundamental value: To be truthful.

14. *Play worst-case scenarios.*

Here the intent is to answer the questions: How bad can things get, and how can we hedge against the worst outcomes? This calls for creative thinking and some speculation. After all, we never have all the facts. There are always uncertainties and assumptions. So, what can we do? We can and must do our best, recognizing the difficulty of the task, and knowing we cannot with certainty predict outcomes.

Why is it so hard? Perhaps it's because we do not want to look at the most uncomfortable negative assumptions that alone will let us see the worse-case outcomes. But the leader must do it. Our cases provide good examples of the value of asking "what-if" questions and the folly of not asking them.

- In the *Cuban Missile Crisis*, two questions proved particularly important: If we bomb Cuba, can we take out all the missiles and, if we bomb or invade, what will the Soviets do? Concern over the answers to both these questions eventually led to the successful blockade strategy.

- The *U2 Crisis* may be the best illustration of the folly of not asking certain obvious questions: What is the likelihood we will be caught in a lie? And what might happen if we are? If Eisenhower had posed these questions seriously to his advisors, this incident would probably have been handled quite differently.

- In the *Corporate Malfeasance Crisis*, as the highly respected *Arthur Anderson* accounting firm repeatedly compromised the auditing function to retain consulting clients, one wonders if anyone at the top asked: What happens to us and our clients if we get caught? It's a good bet that this was never made the subject of serious discussion at a board meeting.

15. *Take a long-term view.*

Crises bite us in the present. They scream for action. Usually, all kinds of pressures are put on the leader—to act—to do something NOW. Short-term actions are important in a crisis—to stop what's happening, to prevent things from getting worse, and at times to simply make people feel better about a disturbing situation. But the leader has an additional mandate: to consider the long-term implications of proposed actions.

- Johnson & Johnson's actions during the *Tylenol Crisis* were always guided by its desired long-term outcome: a reputation for social responsibility.

- The *U2 Crisis*, the *Catholic Church Crisis*, the *Corporate Malfeasance Crisis*, and *Memogate* are all examples of how crises deepen when leaders fail to consider the long-term implications of short-term actions.

16. *Don't act on impulse—stay calm.*

Crises generate pressure on the leader. One's instinct is to reduce the pressure through prompt action. And timely action is usually required. But the leader must walk the fine line between appropriately prompt action and impulsive reaction.

Calmness in crises is essential, and it must start with the leader. Confusion is contagious. It stresses everyone, causing risky recommendations by staff and bad decisions by leaders.

- In the *Cuban Missile Crisis*, if Kennedy had followed the first instincts of his team, he would have attacked Cuba with bombs and troops. Had he done so, the Soviets might have used the tactical nuclear weapons we now know they had. Kennedy's cool head led him and his team to a more reasonable and ultimately correct decision.

- In *Memogate*, the impulse to get the story out clouded judgment. And the lack of a calm assessment of their situation led to the protracted CBS defense of the story, which deepened the crisis.

17. *State objectives clearly.*

Nothing is so important as the leader's voice in crises. And no message from the leader is more important than his or her statement of objectives. It informs multiple audiences and gives marching orders to the team and the total organization. Two historical examples of clear inspirational objectives come to mind: President Roosevelt after Pearl Harbor ("unconditional surrender") and Churchill in the darkest days of World War II ("Our goal is victory, victory at all costs").

Our cases here provide both good and bad examples:

- In the *Cuban Missile Crisis*, Kennedy had a very clear objective: Get the missiles out of Cuba without a war. His speech to the country and the world on Day #7 of the crisis clearly articulated this objective.

- The *Tylenol Crisis* is an example of the wisdom of leaders articulating a message to protect the public.

- The *Corporate Malfeasance Case* shows what can happen when leaders fail to develop or clearly articulate ethical mission statements.

Your Turn

Of the five principles for developing a course of action in a crisis, which two do you consider the most important? Why?

Implementing the Plan

18. *React in a timely way.*

Caution is the watchword in applying this principle. Crises often require immediate actions. However, sometimes delay is advisable in either acknowledging the existence of a crisis or in implementing first actions. The senior leader's task is to know when to wait and when to act.

> "It is what you learn after you know it all that counts."
>
> —John Wooden
> Hall of Fame
> Basketball Coach

- President Kennedy's orchestration of events during the thirteen days of the *Cuban Missile Crisis* is instructive. He did not immediately reveal to the Soviets that we knew about the missiles. He knew he had about ten days before they would be operational, and he wanted to use part of that time to fully explore his options. He waited until Day #7 of the crisis to inform Congress and the world of his intentions. In this case, timing was critical. The delay gave the ExComm time to debate the options and move ultimately to recommend the blockade. If forced to an earlier recommendation, it might have chosen some combination of bombing and invasion.

- Johnson & Johnson took a different approach in the *Tylenol Crisis*, and rightly so. They saw the urgency, put the public interest first, and immediately recalled the contaminated capsules.

- In *Memogate*, CBS would have significantly limited the damage had executives promptly admitted the mistake.

19. *Carefully prepare your first public statement.*

The leader's first public statement in a crisis sets the stage for all that follows. Some important "musts" that should guide first statements are:

- Be clear.

- Keep it simple.

- Be truthful—the truth will ultimately come out.

- Acknowledge any responsibility for the crisis.

- Divulge the facts to the extent you can within the constraints of legal and security considerations.

- Identify what you don't know.

- State what you are doing to get the facts and to deal with the crisis.

- Specify how you will continue to communicate.

- Be careful of your rhetoric. Humiliating others may, on rare occasions, be appropriate—but it is usually counterproductive.

Our cases here, plus a few other historical examples, illustrate the impact of both good and bad first public statements.

- President Nixon's televised denial in the Watergate crisis, President Clinton's in the Monica Lewinsky case, and the awkward way Dan Rather initially defended the *Memogate* story did as much as anything to cost them public support when the truth came out.

- In the *U2 Crisis* it was a succession of false statements that got Eisenhower into trouble.

- Kennedy's prompt public acknowledgment of his mistakes saved his presidency after the *Bay of Pigs* disaster. And his statement during the *Cuban Missile Crisis* was carefully designed to not humiliate Khrushchev.

20. *Continuously expand communications linkages.*

Communications linkages are the leader's lifelines in crises, needed for intelligence and for exchanges with each constituency and with adversaries. The leader cannot have too many sources of information and channels of communications. Plus, one can never tell when some links will shut down. Hence the advice: Continuously expand them.

Of all our cases, the *Cuban Missile Crisis* provides the best illustration of this principle. Here are a few of the many communications linkages used:

- The most obvious link was direct communications between Kennedy and Khrushchev via teletype. There was no telephone hotline between them at the time. However, one was established after the crisis.

- On the third day of the crisis, the President had a scheduled meeting with Soviet Foreign Minister Andrei Gromyko. When the subject of Cuba came up, Gromyko assured the President there were no offensive missiles there. Kennedy did not tell Gromyko he knew about the missiles in Cuba, but he used the opportunity to tell Gromyko that "the gravest issues would arise" if offensive missiles were discovered.

- Twice, at critical times during the thirteen days, the President sent his brother Robert to convey a message to Robert's friend, Russian Ambassador Dobrynin.

- Late in the crisis, a communications link between the U.S. journalist John Scali and Soviet KGB Station Chief Aleksandra Fomin was exploited to exchange ideas with the Soviets on a way to resolve the crisis.

- On Day #10 of the crisis, the U.S. Ambassador to the United Nations communicated the story of the crisis to the world, offering conclusive photographic evidence.

21. *Recognize no long-term secrecy is possible.*

The leader is often confronted with the task of balancing secrecy with the public's right to know. But in designing an information plan, the leader must keep in mind two facts: You cannot keep a crisis situation secret for long, and the truth will eventually come out.

- Nixon with Watergate, Clinton with Monica Lewinsky, Eisenhower with the *U2*, Kennedy with the *Bay of Pigs*, and CBS with *Memogate*— all are examples of leaders failing to recognize that the truth would ultimately surface and hurt them.

- The *Catholic bishops* should have realized early-on that their problem could not be kept from the public forever. The eventual and inevitable public surfacing of the facts led to the ever deepening crisis.

- Johnson & Johnson had it right: Face the facts. Tell it all. Tell it now.

22. *Promptly acknowledge mistakes and correct mis-statements.*

People forgive mistakes and mis-statements, but only if the leader is forth-coming early-on and tells the full story. This is one of the most obvious lessons of history. Yet it seems to be the hardest for leaders to learn.

- Had Nixon immediately told the full story of Watergate, he would never have been forced to resign.

- Clinton was not impeached for his relations with an intern—but for lying about it under oath.

- At any point in the trail of lies following the shooting down of the *U2* plane, Eisenhower could have brought the crisis to a close by telling the truth.

- Had the *Catholic bishops* openly acknowledged the sexual abuse problems in the Church early, and announced corrective actions, they might have avoided their crisis situation.

- Kennedy's prompt public acceptance of responsibility for the mistakes made in the *Bay of Pigs invasion* minimized the impact of those mistakes. Handled with less candor, this misadventure could have seriously damaged his reputation at home and abroad.

- Had CBS been as quick and candid in *Memogate*, the damage to the corporation would have been considerably reduced.

23. *Stay focused.*

Particularly in a crisis of long duration, it is easy to lose focus. Leaders must guard against this and remain focused—and demonstrate that focus in their public statements.

- We can read all the statements of Churchill during the years of World War II and the message never varied: Stand up to Hitler at all costs.

- The U.S. policy in World War II was stated early as "unconditional surrender." There were times along the way when a settlement might have been reached had we settled for less. Some, to this day, feel we should have—and that's ok. But the lesson here is the power of focus. Those two words guided our policy and actions throughout the war.

- We can differ in our opinion of the Bush Doctrine, but it does clearly provide focus in the war on terror: We go after terrorists of global reach and countries that support them. That doctrine has guided our every action since 9/11.

24. *Balance tenacity with flexibility.*

A natural corollary to the need for focus is that the leader must be tenacious in pursuit of the objective. But it is also true that circumstances can change, and the leader must be alert for opportunities to solve the crisis through a shift in focus.

- During the *Cuban Missile Crisis* Kennedy established an arc of 800 miles around Cuba and announced that the United States would stop and board any Soviet ship penetrating that boundary. On the eighth day of the crisis, as Soviet ships approached the arc, Kennedy, against the advice of many, contracted the arc from 800 to 500 miles. His flexibility in giving his opponent more latitude and more time is now credited with preventing a possible escalation of the crisis.

- The bishops in the *Catholic Church Crisis* were tenacious in their efforts to keep their problems out of the public eye. But as the number of offenses grew, they should have recognized the futility of this strategy and had the flexibility to change it.

25. *Stay calm.*

This is an important quality of a leader anytime, but it is never more important than during crises. The leader needs that inner calm to think clearly and conserve energy. More importantly, panic is contagious. The leader must set the example for the whole team—sometimes a whole organization or other nations.

History provides us countless examples:

- Churchill leading England as it stood alone against Hitler.
- Roosevelt reassuring a nation in a deep financial depression, and in a world war.
- Kennedy trying to negotiate his way out of a nuclear war.
- Bush in the immediate aftermath of 9/11.

26. *Follow through and learn as you go.*

An earlier principle emphasized the need to be mindful of history. If leaders practiced that principle, if they studied the crises of the past, they would learn much about what works and what doesn't in a crisis.

But they would not learn it all, could not learn enough. Every crisis is different—in setting, in substance, in players. So often critical learning must be acquired *from* the crisis, *during* the crisis.

Learning doesn't happen by accident. Particularly in the midst of the sometimes frantic activity of a crisis, it is hard to stop and ask: What have we learned about this crisis thus far that could guide our next actions and our handling of other crises in the future?

- Had they been looking over a multi-decade period, the bishops would have seen that, in spite of the advice of doctors, rehabilitation and transfer of sex offenders does not work.
- If one considers U.S. relations with Cuba throughout the Kennedy administration as one continual crisis, then we can see that Kennedy learned critical lessons from the failed *Bay of Pigs* incident that helped

him during the *Cuban Missile Crisis*: have a healthy skepticism about military advice, and get out of the way of your advisors when they are developing action recommendations.

-   One can only hope that business leaders of the future will search earnestly for the lessons learned from the *Corporate Malfeasance Crisis*.

<u>Your Turn</u>

Of the nine principles for implementing the crisis management plan, which three do you consider most important? Why?

Summary

- Crises:
    - Are always looming for organizations
    - Can threaten the organization's survival or prosperity
    - Must and can be managed
- Certain principles help, such as:
    - Assemble the right team
    - Never assume you have the full facts
    - Be true to your values
    - Play worst-case scenarios
    - Don't act on impulse—stay calm
- The principles form a framework or lens to view the crisis and manage it.
- The lens is the tool; using it to guide action is the technique.

Application Exercises

Exercise #1: Personal Assessment of Crisis Management Skills

Try to answer the following five questions as a process of self-development in the crisis management skill area:

1. How would you rate yourself as a crisis manager?

2. How do you know? In what ways have you been tested?

3. How would colleagues rate you as a crisis manager?

4. What weaknesses do you have in this skill area?

5. What actions could you take to improve your capacity to manage crisis?

Thoughts on the Exercise

- This exercise asks you to rate yourself as a crisis manager. But it does more: It forces you to validate your opinion by examining the ways your skills have been tested in the past. Further, it asks you to think about how others might rate you as a crisis manager.

- Perhaps the most important part of this exercise is the requirement to identify your weaknesses as a crisis manager and develop specific actions to correct those weaknesses.

- Actions might include simply willing yourself to behave in a different way in crises (easier to do once you have identified a weakness). Another action might be to study the subject of crisis management in more detail, using both theoretical texts and true accounts of individuals in crisis.

Exercise #2: Your Assessment of the Crisis Management Principles

Examine the principles of crisis management, with your own experience and knowledge in mind. Circle those principles that you feel are particularly important. Pick the five you consider the most important. Finally, add any principles that you consider important but don't find on the list. *Note*: In doing this exercise it might be helpful to think of major crises that you have observed or read about—these are certainly part of your experience.

Thoughts on the Exercise

- The purpose of this exercise is to help you bring your own experiences to the topic of crisis management. You are asked first to identify the most important principles from the author's list—then to add additional principles suggested from your own experience.

- This is not an invitation to ignore principles you consider to be of lower priority—but merely a technique to make you think about your own knowledge and experience with crises.

Part IV

Willingness to Accept Risk

"To conquer without risk is to triumph without glory."

—Pierre Corneille
(Le Cid ([1636], Act II, Sc. ii)

"Risk must be evaluated not by the fear it generates in you or the probability of your success, but by the value of the goal."

—John C. Maxwell

"Courage is the greatest of all the virtues. Because if you haven't courage, you may not have an opportunity to use any of the others."

—Samuel Johnson

This module is designed to help the reader understand why a willingness to accept risks is a critical component of the senior leader's skill set.

When boards pick leaders, or leaders accept positions, it is important that both consider what difficult tasks and decisions confront the organization. A leader may have all the other "right" skills and qualities. But if he or she is not willing to accept the personal risks involved in doing what is necessary, then that person cannot lead the organization.

Much is written in the management literature about environmental scanning and other approaches for identifying and reducing risks. And risk management *is* important. But the focus here is on another quality: *The capacity of the leader to fully appreciate a serious risk, and to press on in the face of that risk.* In short, if leaders are unwilling to face the inevitable risks that go with troubled times, they will not have the nerve to take action—and thus they will fail.

Chapter 8 (Four Risk Takers—Their Stories and Impact) identifies various types of risks that leaders may face and illustrates the leader's dilemma through the true stories of four leaders: Katherine Graham, Martin Luther King, Pope John XXIII, and President John F. Kennedy. Taken collectively, these four cases highlight the importance of risk tolerance—in diverse organizational settings and leadership situations.

The chapter begins with learning objectives and ends with summary points. At the end of each of the four cases, a "Your Turn" question is posed to help you reflect on the material and relate it to your experience.

The best way to navigate this module is to first read the chapter. After reading each case, reflect on the "Your Turn" question. Next, reflect again on the chapter objectives and summary. And finally, complete the application exercises.

What result should you expect? A clearer understanding of the relationship of risk tolerance to executive performance and a better appreciation of your own personal attitude toward risk.

Chapter 8

Four Risk Takers—Their Stories and Impact

Objectives

- Recognize the types of risks faced by senior leaders.
- Learn the stories of four senior leaders who took severe risks.
- Understand why a senior leader must be willing to accept risk.
- Understand your own tolerance for risk.

There are many types of risks to the leader in difficult times:

-	Failure	—Inability to succeed in one's job
-	Firing	—Involuntary loss of one's job
-	Reputation	—Failure to live up to previous performance or expectations
-	Re-election	—Loss of a political position
-	Health	—Illness due to job stress or environmental health hazards
-	Personal Safety	—Risk due to threats or dangerous work
-	Family Safety	—Risk to family due to threats
-	Financial Security	—Risk of one's personal financial assets

To validate the importance of a leader's risk tolerance, four case examples are provided—stories of leaders who took a risk to lead well:

-	Katherine Graham	—Risked her company (*The Washington Post*) to expose President Nixon during the Watergate crisis.

- Martin Luther King   —Risked his life to lead his movement.
- Pope John XXIII   —Risked alienating the Catholic Church hierarchy in Rome and many Catholics to modernize his church.
- President John F. Kennedy   —Risked losing the South in his bid for re-election by publicly supporting the black minority in the civil rights struggle.

These examples were chosen not only because each leader was faced with very real and serious risks, but with the goal of balance in mind: One case is from business, one from government, one from the non-profit sector, and one is from leadership of a social movement.

Katherine Graham and Watergate
(Risking the Company)

The Watergate affair started with a bungled attempt by Republican operatives to break in and bug the offices of the Democratic National Committee on June 17, 1972.

Initially, the White House simply denied involvement and tried to characterize the event as a burglary of little importance. But it proved to be the tip of a destructive iceberg that would sink the Nixon presidency.

The investigation of this event ultimately exposed a broad array of illegal activities committed to help Richard Nixon win re-election in 1972. Illegalities included disruption of the political processes of the country, infringements on civil liberties, misuse of campaign funds, and the use of government agencies (e.g., FBI, CIA, and IRS) to harm political opponents. Watergate is considered the worst political scandal in our nation's history. Over thirty Nixon administration and campaign officials as well as campaign contributors were either convicted of breaking the law or pleaded guilty to charges. The President, facing certain impeachment, resigned on August 9, 1974, when evidence clearly revealed he was involved in the attempt to cover up his administration's involvement in the scandal.

To lead is often to leap in the dark

"Behold the turtle. He makes progress only when he sticks his neck out."

—James Bryant Conant

During the two-year investigation, the President and his press secretary insisted repeatedly that no members of the White House staff were involved. That the truth was eventually uncovered was a tribute to many individuals and groups: special prosecutors, the Senate Watergate Committee, the House Impeachment Committee, and a tough U.S. District Court Judge (John J. Sirica), who demanded Nixon turn over crucial tapes of conversations that established his complicity in the cover-up.

However, during that long two-year period, the story was kept alive for the public mainly by one newspaper: The *Washington Post. The Post* was able to play this pivotal role in exposing illegalities and bringing down a president through the skill and tenacity of two investigative reporters (Carl Bernstein and Bob Woodward) and the courage of its editor (Ben Bradlee) and its owner and publisher, Katherine Graham—who literally risked her company by supporting them.

There were a variety of ways the President could retaliate against *The Post*, and there were warnings by high ranking officials that the administration would indeed play hardball. Proof soon followed in the form of restricted access, unusual challenges to TV license renewals by the Federal Communications Commission (FCC), and even rumors of physical danger to *Post* personnel. Additionally, there was always the risk to reputation of being wrong at the top of one's lungs.

The Post felt the pressure. Ben Bradlee said in his autobiography: "We felt as if we were in a constant, high-stakes pitched battle. If we lost, a great newspaper's reputation would suffer mortal injuries...and all of us would be looking for work." Nor is there any doubt that Graham personally understood the risk she was taking by supporting her reporters and editor. She said in her Pulitzer Prize-winning autobiography: "I have to admit that I was frightened. I was frightened of the power of a man and his minions, of a President who thought he had the power to wrap himself in the cloak of national security. I was frightened for the future of The Washington Post Company."

But Katherine Graham led by taking the risk—and she prevailed. *The Post* became known as a world-class newspaper through its role in Watergate. Further, Graham emerged as a true leader in the field of journalism. In an editorial in *U.S. News and World Report*, following her death in July 2001, David Gergen wrote:

> "Whenever you see a successful business, someone once made a courageous decision."
>
> —Peter Drucker

"Her courage in publishing the Pentagon Papers and in sticking by her troops as they pursued Watergate not only transformed *The Post* but set a standard for integrity and excellence that stiffened the backbone of the entire profession."

Graham's dilemma was clear: To lead her company, she had to risk its survival. She did—and won!

Your Turn

Suppose Woodward and Bernstein had been the victims of bad information. How much of a problem would this have been for Graham? Do you think she felt at risk of being wrong?

Pope John XXIII

(Risking Significant Internal Conflict)

The story of Pope John XXIII is an example of the skillful implementation of radical change—by a leader with a far-reaching vision and the courage to face determined resistance and some alienated constituencies to advance that vision.

The Pope's goals were to bring the Catholic Church more in tune with the times and reconcile all Christians. His approach to achieve these goals was to convene the Second Vatican Council (Vatican II): A meeting of the 3000 bishops of the Church from around the world.

> Stick to your guns when you know you are right.

> "If we are called to great ends, we are called to great hazards."
>
> —John Henry Cardinal Newman

Vatican II was convened in October 1962. It was only the twentieth such gathering in 2000 years, the first since 1869, and only the second since the Council of Trent in 1545. So—it was obviously an event of monumental importance.

The changes in the Catholic Church resulting from Vatican II can only be regarded as revolutionary: They reshaped the Church and its relations to other religions and the world, changed the liturgy of the Mass, gave local bishops and the laity expanded roles in church functions and leadership, and went far to heal divisions between Catholics and non-Catholics.

Specific outcomes of the Council included:

- Use of local languages in the Mass (previously only said in Latin).

- A decentralization of the authority of Rome: The Church seen as a community of local churches with local bishops sharing in the overall church leadership.

- A sense of the Church as more than just the hierarchy, clergy, and religious. Acknowledgment that the laity too should have a role as direct participants in the mission of the Church.

- Greater outreach to other religions through the ecumenical movement and an acknowledgment that all religions offer a path to God—that the Catholic Church is not the only means of salvation.

- Rejection of the long-held view that the Jews bore moral responsibility for the death of Christ.

-    Acknowledgment that there is a hierarchy of truths—that not all official church teachings are equally binding or essential to the integrity of the Catholic faith.

Such wide-ranging change is not brought about easily, and John XXIII suffered no delusions about the difficulty of his task. He decided to convene the Council soon after becoming Pope in 1958. But when he proposed it to the members of the Roman Curia (the Vatican's central governing body), he met with significant opposition as they tried to persuade him to abandon, or at least delay, calling the Council.

The Pope was faced with a centralized power structure. The Curia was in charge of all aspects of church life. Further, most of its members were conservatives who were opposed to anything that might threaten their authority or what they considered to be the good traditions of the Church. The Pope knew from the outset that confronting the Curia meant swimming upstream, and he was right. He had to fight the initial opposition to the Council and the continual efforts of the Curia and many bishops throughout the world to achieve dominance of their views throughout the three years of the Council.

The Pope recognized clearly his own position in this struggle: He had absolute authority to do what he wanted. He could have simply imposed his will on the Curia and the Church. But this was not his way. John XXIII was a very sophisticated diplomat

> "Only those who dare to fail greatly can ever achieve greatly."
>
> —Robert F. Kennedy

and a skilled leader. He recognized the need to influence others to bring about lasting change. He accepted this challenge and its risks.

The Pope accepted two major risks in calling the Council and pushing such an ambitious agenda. First, there was the opposition of the bureaucracy in Rome, which he knew would try to derail any efforts to change the status quo. This opposition was a threat to the outcome of the Council. Second, there was the risk that the outcomes of the Council would alienate the sizeable minority of very conservative Catholics worldwide. It took courage to proceed in the face of these risks. But John XXIII knew what he wanted to accomplish—and he sensed that the time was right. And time has proven his judgment correct. At the Council, he was helped by a force the Curia had not counted on: strong support by the more liberal elements—bishops empowered by the very existence of the Council. In the end, the Pope and those who shared the same vision won the battle with those who feared the risks and the threat to their power. The Pope got the changes he sought.

The changes were welcomed by people of other religions and by the vast majority of Catholics, who saw the Council's decisions and directions as progressive and timely. As anticipated, there was opposition by many who feared change—an opposition that continues to this day.

The long-term impact of Vatican II has led to concerns in some circles. Some feel the Council has produced a degree of liberalism that goes beyond its original intent. Others worry that Vatican II, by replacing many certainties of the faith with ambiguities, has confused and disturbed many sincere Catholics.

But the fact remains: The Catholic Church was forever changed in major ways by Vatican II. And this change would have been impossible without the diplomatic skill and determination of one man: Pope John XXIII—and by his courage to accept the risks inherent in such a major undertaking.

Your Turn

How do you think Pope John XXIII would have handled the sex abuse crisis in the Catholic Church?

Martin Luther King, Jr.

(Risking Life for a Cause)

The purpose here is not to describe in detail the history of race relations in the United States. The long period of slavery, brought to an end by the Civil War, is well known. Still, at the beginning of the 20th century, deep racial prejudice existed in the United States, sometimes even continued as a matter of law: "Jim Crow" laws in the South barred blacks from white-only schools and just about every other public facility. Literacy tests, pole taxes, and obscure "grandfather clauses" (excluding anyone whose grandfather had not voted) prevented most blacks from voting.

In the famous *Plessy vs. Ferguson* case (1896) the U.S. Supreme Court had upheld the segregation of public facilities and services provided they were "separate and equal."

In both world wars, blacks served in the armed forces, but always in separate/segregated units. That practice ended on July 26, 1948, when President Truman issued Executive Order 9981 requiring "equality of treatment and opportunity to all persons in the armed services without regard to race."

However, at mid-century, for most citizens, particularly in the South, deep prejudice remained, and facilities and services remained separate but clearly not equal. But change was in the air and two events gave change a push:

- On May 17, 1954, the U.S. Supreme Court handed down a landmark decision in the case of *Brown vs. Board of Education of Topeka, Kansas*. NAACP lawyers convinced the high court that segregated schools were inherently unequal—and the court's decision made desegregation of the nation's schools the new law of the land. Integration wasn't easy, but the process was started.

- On December 1, 1955, a black woman (Rosa Parks), tired from her day's work, boarded a city bus in Montgomery, Alabama, sat in the front (white section) and refused the driver's order to move to the rear (black section). This was a violation of the law, and Parks was arrested. That arrest resulted in a year-long boycott by Montgomery's black citizens and ultimately in the desegregation of the Montgomery buses. More importantly, it brought civil rights to the attention of the whole country—and it gave rise to a new civil rights leader: Martin Luther King, Jr.

Martin Luther King at the time was the young pastor of Dexter Avenue Baptist Church in Montgomery. He was recognized as a leader and was asked to serve as president of the organization formed to run the boycott.

A necessary and great cause warrants any risk.

King was inspired by the leadership model of India's great leader, Mahatma Gandhi: nonviolent civil disobedience. In his first speech to his colleagues, King struck a chord that guided all his subsequent actions through his years of civil rights leadership.

"One never finds anything perfectly pure and...exempt from danger."

—Niccolo Machiavelli

> "First and foremost, we are American citizens.... We are not here advocating violence...the only weapon that we have...is the weapon of protest...the great glory of American democracy is the right to protest for right."

Throughout the many events that marked King's movement there were threats—ample to discourage any ordinary person. But King was no ordinary man.

Given his long period of leadership and the level of national violence during that time, it would have been understandable, excusable, and perhaps even wise to step down—to spare his family if not himself from the constant danger.

But Martin Luther King had his vision, his "dream." And he recognized that he brought skilled and inspirational leadership to his movement. He said to those gathered outside his house after it was bombed on January 30, 1956: "If I am stopped, our work will not stop. For what we are doing is right." Yes, surely the movement would have gone on without him, but

"It is only by risking our persons from one hour to another that we live at all."

—William James

probably in a more violent and less effective way. King, in the midst of violence always kept people calm. Again, in his remarks after the bombing, he told his followers: "We believe in law and order. Don't get panicky. Don't do anything panicky at all. Don't get your weapons." King knew it was not just about moving forward in civil rights, but doing it peacefully. He also knew he was the leader with the best chance of making that happen.

Was he conscious of the risks to himself and his family? Certainly. Who could doubt that, given all the violence and threats during that period? But he came to grips with it early. In his autobiography, he described his sleepless night after the 1956 bombing, of the suggestions of others to get bodyguards and armed watchmen for his house. But King thought it through and decided he could not serve as leader of a nonviolent movement and still use weapons, even to protect himself and his family.

King got rid of his only gun at that time and adopted a fearless philosophy for the remaining twelve years of his life. In his autobiography, he explains that philosophy: "I was much more afraid in Montgomery when I had a gun in my house. When I decided that I couldn't keep a gun, I came face-to-face with the question of death and I dealt with it. From that point on, I no longer needed a gun nor have I been afraid. Had we become distracted by the question of my safety, we would have lost the moral offensive and sunk to the level of our oppressors."

King knew that to lead his movement he had to accept the risks to his life. Shot and killed in Memphis, Tennessee, on April 4, 1968, he lost his gamble with risk. But his cause has endured. His leadership changed the country for good, forever.

Your Turn

Martin Luther King not only put his own life at risk but also the lives of his family members. Would you be willing to take such a risk?

President John F. Kennedy
(Risking Re-election for Civil Rights)

This is the story of strong leadership by President John F. Kennedy in the face of huge political risks. The date was June 11, 1963. The issue was civil rights.

The early 1960s had seen increased civil rights activism: Freedom rides, marches and demonstrations, sit-ins, and boycotts had increased the country's awareness of the state of inequality that existed between black and white citizens, particularly in the South.

But it took the events in Birmingham, Alabama, in April and May 1963, to force action by the federal government. Picketing and store sit-ins triggered violent action by the Birmingham police under the leadership of Police Commissioner Eugene "Bull" Connor. Over 2000 people were jailed, and dogs and fire hoses were directed against street demonstrators. The American public was rightly outraged.

Until this time, President Kennedy, while privately in sympathy with the black community, had not publicly committed to their cause. He had held back partly for political reasons: He needed the South in a re-election bid and the support of Southern members in Congress.

An event on June 11, 1963, and a persuasive argument by Vice President Lyndon Johnson moved him to action—to finally officially put the federal government on the side of the blacks in the civil rights struggle, in spite of the personal political risks involved. That day, Alabama Governor George Wallace personally stood in the door of the University of Alabama at Tuscaloosa to bar the registration of two black students. As a result, Kennedy had to federalize the Alabama National Guard to achieve their admission to the university.

According to Kennedy biographer Richard Reeves, it was Vice President Johnson who convinced Kennedy on that day to fully commit the federal government to the black minority in the civil rights struggle. In a chapter on Kennedy in the book, *Character Above All*, edited by Robert A. Wilson, Reeves writes: "Johnson told him that the black-white problem was escalating in the country because as long as the President did not take a position, either with the majority white or the minority black, both sides believed that, in his heart, the President was with them." Johnson convinced him that to reduce the level of conflict, he would have to take a side.

Reeves reports: "Kennedy accepted that argument. He went on television that night and in another great speech, done largely without notes, he said: This is not a political question, this is a moral question. This is a question of

> It's never too late to do the right thing.

what kind of people we are. And if we do believe in equality, then who among us would choose to be black?"

Kennedy ended his speech with this commitment: "I am, therefore, asking Congress to enact legislation giving all Americans the right to be served in facilities which are open to the public—hotels, restaurants, theaters, retail stores, and similar establishments." In this statement he also asked Congress to authorize government participation in lawsuits designed to end segregation in public education—and he added that other features would also be requested, including greater protection for the right to vote.

> "Don't be afraid to take a big step if one is indicated. You can't cross a chasm in two small steps."
>
> —David Lloyd George

Writing about character in *Character Above All*, Reeves says of this day, this speech: "Whatever character is, John Kennedy had it that day." And so he did! We'll never know if this act would have cost him the South in a re-election campaign. But we do know he was willing to risk that loss in the interest of leading his country to higher ground. And he could not have led this cause without being willing to accept the risk.

> "A man does what he must—in spite of personal consequences, in spite of obstacles and dangers and pressures—and that is the basis of all morality."
>
> —John F. Kennedy

Your Turn

Kennedy and Johnson did not have a very warm relationship. Why do you suppose Kennedy listened to him on this matter?

The four cases just discussed illustrate the importance of a leader's willingness to accept risks. Had these four individuals been unwilling to face the risk, they would simply not have been able to accomplish their leadership task—because they would not have attempted that task.

History offers many other examples of leaders making bold moves in the face of high risks.

- President Truman's decision to drop atomic bombs on Japan might have resulted in some form of international condemnation. And he knew his decision to fire General Douglas MacArthur would hurt his own popularity at home.

- President Gerald Ford knew he was risking re-election by pardoning Richard Nixon.

- Edward R. Morrow risked his job and reputation by his attack on the powerful Senator Joseph McCarthy in the anti-communism frenzy of the early 1950s.

- Walter Cronkite risked his credibility, popularity, and access to government when he publicly turned against the Vietnam War.

- Lee Iacocca risked his reputation when he assumed leadership of a failing Chrysler Corporation.

The evidence is abundant and clear. Generals who make bold moves like splitting their forces and abandoning supply lines, leaders of expeditions with serious risks to life, astronauts facing the unknown in space—these leaders would not attempt, much less achieve, their goals were they not willing to face the risks. Therefore, I think the case is clear: Willingness to accept risk deserves a place in the senior leader's set of required qualities.

Summary

- Bold leadership actions always involve personal risks to the leader.
- The risks may threaten such things as:
    - Job security
    - Reputation
    - Re-election
    - Personal safety
    - Financial security
- Senior leaders must develop a high tolerance for risk—or, regardless of their other talents, they may fail through lack of nerve to act.

Application Exercises

Exercise #1: Assessing Your Risk Tolerance

Below are some of the risks that senior leaders sometimes must take to effectively lead their organizations:

Failure in a job

Firing from a job

Loss of reputation

Political re-election failure

Health risk

Personal safety risk

Risk to family safety or security

Financial loss

Check any of the risks that would cause you to reconsider accepting a leadership position. List any other risks (not on the list) that might cause you to reconsider.

Thoughts on the Exercise

There are no right or wrong answers to this exercise. It simply provides a framework to assist you in identifying the areas of risk that commonly confront top leaders and your own tolerance for these risks.

Exercise #2: A Reflection on Leaders Taking Risks

Think back over your experiences and answer these four questions:

1. Have you ever observed a senior leader confront a risk that he or she did not anticipate?
2. What was the organization, situation, and risk?
3. How did the leader react?
4. What was the outcome for the organization and the individual?

Thoughts on the Exercise

This exercise asks you to enter the world of risk-taking by reflecting on some leader's performance in a risky environment. *Note*: If you have difficulty thinking of a leader you have personally observed, use a historical example for this exercise.

Appendix

Suggestions for Teachers and Trainers

One of the purposes of this book is to serve as a resource for teachers and trainers. This appendix is designed to assist in that purpose by offering suggestions for classroom use. Specifically, the appendix suggests individual and group projects for each of the four parts or modules, plus questions for homework assignments or to stimulate classroom discussion.

First, a few general thoughts for *teachers*. Although the book might be considered a stand-alone text for a short seminar on senior leadership, it is best suited as a resource for the *senior-level leadership segment* of a graduate course in management or leadership.

Since the material would likely be covered in about 20 to 30 percent of the overall course, it is suggested that lecturing be held to a minimum—that students learn the concepts by reading the book and that class time be used for projects, exercises, and discussion.

With this idea in mind, two sets of resources are provided here (for each of the four parts): (1) Individual and group projects, and (2) discussion questions.

The individual and group projects can be used, as written, for college courses, but they may need to be modified for training seminars. The trainer's job often comes with limitations: Instruction time may be much shorter, students may not have time to read the book, and homework may not be possible. So, *trainers* may need to lecture on the concepts and modify projects to fit the constraints of each training situation.

Part I: Characteristics and Qualities

Individual and Group Projects

Project #1

Students are asked to come to class with a list of the three professional characteristics and three personal qualities in which they feel they need the most improvement—and some actions they feel would help them improve in those areas. In class, students discuss their findings in subgroups and get peer advice. Subgroups report major insights to the whole class.

Project #2

Students read the biography or autobiography of a leader picked by the instructor. Each student comes to class with a critique of the leader on each characteristic and quality—a paper (that could be graded) or simply a set of notes for subgroup discussion. Subgroups select the best ideas from individual papers or notes and produce an oral briefing as their subgroup critique of the leader.

Project #3

Each student picks a leader to critique using the nineteen characteristics and qualities. The subject can be a historical figure or a leader the student has observed personally. Students prepare a briefing for the class on their critique. A graded paper on the subject might be added to this requirement.

Discussion Questions

1. Assume you are a very successful CEO of a large advertising firm, have had no military experience, yet have accepted an appointment as Assistant Secretary of Defense for Manpower. You anticipate that the senior military and career government officials are thinking: "He doesn't have a clue about our world." What would you do to establish credibility in this new job?

2. Examine the list of top executive roles. Have you ever observed a senior leader who lacked the top executive perspective? What problems did that shortcoming cause for the organization?

3. Have you ever witnessed an organization having difficulty developing a vision statement? What was the problem?

4. As a senior leader, what is or what would be your technique for maintaining a sufficient external orientation so as not to get blindsided by something in the external environment?

5. Should an organization's values and strategy remain constant over time, or should they be subjected to periodic review and changed if necessary? How often should strategy be reviewed?

6. Have you ever been placed in a job where you felt over your head from a technical standpoint? How did you feel? What did you do?

7. How good are your listening skills? Are you able to establish a climate for others that encourages them to be candid with you?

8. To what extent does compensation attract and retain talented people?

9. Is there a danger that a leader's attention to management issues will rob subordinates of their initiative?

10. Have you ever observed a senior leader who was not competent or not interested in financial and resources allocation matters? What was the impact on the organization's decision-making process?

11. Do you think that graduate programs in business and public administration can do anything that will stimulate ethical professional behavior in people?

12. How can leaders improve their ability to exercise good judgment?

13. Why must one's approach differ when negotiating with the boss versus negotiating with a peer or subordinate?

14. Can you think of an American business, political, or military leader who caused problems for himself or his cause by being too inflexible?

15. Can you think of an American business, political, or military leader who caused problems for himself or his cause through a lack of tenacity?

16. When confusion reigns and the world seems to be crumbling around them, many leaders lose their effectiveness. Can you think of a leader who was particularly comfortable or uncomfortable in crises?

17. Can nerve be taught to leaders? Can this quality be acquired or enhanced in any way?

18. How can leaders encourage and facilitate the professional development of subordinates?

19. In the book, *Primal Leadership: Realizing the Power of Emotional Intelligence*, the authors make the point that "in grave crisis, all eyes turn to the leader for emotional guidance." Is this desirable? As a leader, would you prefer your people turn inward and act on their best instincts?

Part II: Ability to Manage Change

Individual and Group Projects

Project #1

Students prepare a paper (or notes) describing some change they would like to bring about in an organization of their choice. (It can be a true or fictional situation.)

Using the nine principles of change to guide their thinking, the students describe the actions they would take to bring about the desired change.

Each student briefs his or her paper (or notes) to subgroup members for discussion and feedback. Subgroups pick the best submission for presentation (by the author) to the whole class.

Project #2

Students prepare a paper describing some organizational change effort they have observed, and critique it using the nine principles of change. They submit the paper for grade and prepare a formal oral briefing to the class on their analysis.

Project #3

The instructor gives students a short fictional situation involving a proposed change in some familiar generic organization (e.g., college, hospital, retail store). Students spend thirty minutes of class time (using the principles of change) to develop suggested actions to facilitate the change. They share their ideas in subgroup discussions that conclude with subgroup reports to the class.

Discussion Questions

1. Can you cite an example from your experience of a change that went well because the organization was alert to all its implications?
2. Can you cite an example from your experience of a change that went poorly because the leader did not remain sufficiently involved?
3. Explain your personal concept of change theory. Why is change theory helpful in managing change?

4. Can you cite an example from your experience of a change that was helped by external forces or trends?

5. Do you think it is easier for leaders to implement change in autocratic cultures or collegial cultures?

6. Have you ever failed to develop validating evidence to support a proposed change? What happened?

7. Have you ever seen a proposed change flounder due to a poor presentation? Explain.

8. Can you cite an example from your experience of a change effort that floundered due to a lack of ongoing evaluation and feedback?

9. Can you cite an example from your experience of a change that went badly because management failed to respond to contingencies that occurred during the change process?

Part III: Ability to Manage Crises

Individual and Group Projects

Project #1

Students prepare a paper describing and critiquing (using the crisis management principles) some real crisis. This can be either a historical crisis they've read about or a crisis they have observed. The papers may be submitted for grade, and the students may also be required to present an oral briefing to the class on their analysis.

Project #2

The instructor picks a crisis that is well-known or well-documented and requires students to critique the management of the crisis using the crisis management principles. Students bring their individual analysis to class (formal paper or simply notes). This individual work is discussed in subgroups. Subgroups integrate the best individual ideas into a subgroup report in the form of a formal briefing or simply comments for full-class discussion.

Discussion Questions

1. Reflect again on the six cases of crisis management discussed: Johnson & Johnson, Corporate Malfeasance, U2 Spy Plane, Cuban Missile Crisis, Memogate, and the Catholic Church Crisis. Which case do you feel is the richest in lessons learned about crisis management?

2. Do you think all the publicity about corporate malfeasance in 2001–2002 and the subsequent prosecution of offenders will have a significant long-term effect on corporate ethics? Explain.

3. Judging by its handling of the Cuban Missile Crisis, how do you think the Kennedy administration would have dealt with the terrorism crisis?

4. Cite some good or bad examples from your personal experience of an organization's efforts to anticipate, prevent, and prepare for crisis?

5. What was the greatest strength and greatest weakness of the Bush team in the handling of the terrorism crisis?

6. What were the three greatest weaknesses of the Catholic Church's approach to organizing and developing a course of action for its crisis?

7. How can leaders ever know if they have reliable facts in a crisis situation? How can they react with confidence if they doubt the reliability of their information?

8. Do you think long-term secrecy can ever be maintained in a crisis situation? How would your view on this matter influence your approach to crisis management?

Part IV: Willingness to Accept Risk

Individual and Group Projects

Project #1

Each student is required to pick a leader who took great risks. This can be a historical figure or a leader personally observed by the student.

Students describe this example of risk-taking in a graded paper and/or an oral briefing to the class.

Project #2

As a variation of project #1, students discuss their risk-taking examples in subgroups. Then the subgroups select the best example and help the author polish the story for an oral presentation in class.

Project #3

Students bring to class their results on Application Exercise #1 (Assessing Your Risk Tolerance). They discuss their results in subgroups to get peer feedback. Subgroups are asked to report a few of the most interesting thoughts expressed during the subgroup discussions.

Discussion Questions

1. Was Katherine Graham's support of her reporters on the Watergate story necessary for the reputation of *The Washington Post*? What would have happened to the paper if Graham had failed to support them? Why do you think she took the risk?

2. In making her decision to support her reporters, Katherine Graham not only put her company at risk, but she was also risking the jobs of all those who worked for *The Washington Post*. Do you think that entered into her decision? Should it have?

3. What was the source of power of Pope John XXIII as he confronted opposition to convening Vatican II?

4. Pope John XXIII died before the completion of Vatican II. Had he lived, say ten years after the last session, what impact do you think that would have had on the Catholic Church?

5. Many leaders, including our presidents, fulfill their leadership roles under the constant threat of assassination. How do you think they manage to deal with such a threat?

6. Was it a bad decision on Martin Luther King's part to refuse protection for himself and/or his family?

7. If John Kennedy were alive today, do you think he would be more proud of his handling of the Cuban Missile crisis or his support of the civil rights struggle? Why?

8. Are there always risks in leading at the top? Explain.

978-0-595-38439-6
0-595-38439-0